PSYCHOLOGY OF EMOTIONS, MOTIVATIONS AND ACTIONS

NEW DEVELOPMENTS IN PERSONALITY DISORDERS RESEARCH

PSYCHOLOGY OF EMOTIONS, MOTIVATIONS AND ACTIONS

Additional books in this series can be found on Nova's website under the Series tab.

Additional e-books in this series can be found on Nova's website under the e-book tab.

PSYCHOLOGY OF EMOTIONS, MOTIVATIONS AND ACTIONS

NEW DEVELOPMENTS IN PERSONALITY DISORDERS RESEARCH

AMELIE MOREL

AND

MICHELLE DURAND

EDITORS

New York

NOTICE TO THE READER

LIBRARY OF CONGRESS CATALOGING-IN-PUBLICATION DATA

New developments in personality disorders research / editors, Amelie Morel and Michelle Durand.
     pages cm
 Includes bibliographical references and index.
 ISBN: 978-1-62417-118-5 (soft cover)
 1. Personality disorders. I. Morel, Amelie. II. Durand, Michelle.
 RC554.N48 2013
 616.85'81--dc23   2012038760

Published by Nova Science Publishers, Inc. ✛ New York

CONTENTS

PREFACE

In this book, the authors discuss new research on personality disorders including grandiose and vulnerable narcissism and the nature of Narcissistic Personality Disorder (NPD); an examination of personality pathology with the five factor model and personality psychopathology-5; forensic and non-forensic mental health nurses' perceptions in relation to their clinical or management focus for those with a diagnostic label of personality/psychopathic disorder; and the Millon Clinical Multiaxial Inventory-III (MCMI-III) and the Personality Disorder Questionnaire-4+ (PDQ-4+) in a mixed Italian psychiatric sample.

Chapter 1 – Narcissism is one of the oldest concepts in psychology, having its roots in Greek mythology and psychodynamic thought. It is studied in both clinical and social/personality psychology, with the clinical literature focusing on Narcissistic Personality Disorder (NPD) and the social/personality literature focusing on trait narcissism. It has been included in the Diagnostic and Statistical Manual of the Mental Disorders (DSM) since the third edition was published in 1980. Alongside clinical theory and research into NPD, research examining the correlates of trait narcissism continues to be popular. This distinguishes two narcissism forms, specifically grandiose (or overt) and vulnerable (or covert) narcissism. Grandiose narcissism is associated with exhibitionism, self-importance, and a preoccupation with receiving attention with others. Vulnerable narcissism is associated with hypersensitivity, anxiety, and insecurity although it is assumed that it is marked by unconscious feelings of grandeur which are proposed to be 'core' common to both forms. Grandiose narcissism is typically assessed using the 40-item Narcissistic Personality Inventory, despite there being no consensus about its factor structure. Several measures of vulnerable narcissism exist, including the 52-item Pathological

Narcissism Scale, that assesses both grandiose and vulnerable narcissism, and the 10-item Hypersensitive Narcissism Inventory (HSNS), which is assumed to be uni-dimensional.

In this chapter, the authors first briefly review the nature of Narcissistic Personality Disorder (NPD) as considered in the various editions and revisions of the DSM. The authors then turn to the measurement of trait narcissism in social/personality psychology, discussing briefly criticisms of the NPI and considering the nature of the PNI and the HSNS. Following this discussion, the authors briefly present the results of our recent studies that have established that the NPI assesses seven distinct correlated dimensions whereas the HSNS assesses two. Both the NPI and the HSNS factor structure is invariant across samples and the NPI factor structure is invariant when different question formats are used. Discussion then focuses on the interrelationships of these factors and their relationships with self-esteem. Following this, the authors consider this etiology, focusing on the propositions of Freud (1914/1957), Kernberg (1975), Kohut (1971, 1977), and Millon (1981). This highlights the role that interactions with caregivers likely play in the etiology of narcissism. Empirical evidence, obtained from two undergraduate samples, for the associations of the higher-order narcissism traits, and their lower-level dimensions, with recollections of cold and overvaluative parenting and with anxious and avoidant attachment is presented. The authors then turn to the role of self-regulation in narcissism, again considering the relationship of the higher-order traits narcissism traits, and their lower level dimensions, with self-regulatory factors, specifically, promotion, prevention, locomotion, and assessment. The chapter closes with the suggestion that research examining lower-level dimensions rather than the higher-level traits provides a better understanding of narcissism.

Chapter 2 – Research suggests that dimensional models are useful in the classification of maladaptive personality traits and that these models are more useful than categorical models. As a result, the personality disorder section of the DSM-5 has proposed a shift from a categorical model to a hybrid dimensional-categorical model of diagnosing personality pathology. The current study will examine the relation between the Personality Psychopathology Five (PSY-5) model of clinically-relevant personality traits taken from the MMPI-2 with the five-factor model (FFM). Participants (n = 22) were recruited from a Psychological Services Center at a Midwestern university. Clinicians working at the center were recruited if they had a client who had previously completed the NEO PI-R and the MMPI-2. The clinicians were asked to complete the Shedler and Western Assessment Procedure

(SWAP-200) to assess their respective client's personality pathology. The current study indicated that both models contribute to our understanding of personality pathology, though conclusions were limited due to the size of the sample.

Chapter 3 – The aim of this study was to compare forensic and non-forensic mental health nurses' perceptions in relation to their clinical or management focus for those with a diagnostic label of personality/psychopathic disorder. The method employed was a postal survey with the distribution of 1490 information gathering schedules across the UK with a response rate of 41.9% of forensic mental health nurses and 76.4% non-forensic mental health nurses being achieved. The results indicate that both groups saw these diagnostic labels more in terms of a management focus ($z = -3.79$; $p<0.01$) rather than a clinical one ($z = -3.53$; $p<0.01$) and that the forensic group scored higher on the management measure ($z = -17.31$; $p<0.01$) in relation to the non-forensic nurses ($z = -11.19$; $p<0.01$). The implications for practice are that nurses who focus more on a management perspective are less likely to facilitate therapeutic change with service users.

Chapter 4 – Self-report questionnaires play a crucial role in the assessment of Personality Disorders (PDs); in such a context, the Millon Clinical Multiaxial Inventory–III (MCMI-III) and the Personality Disorder Questionnaire-4+ (PDQ-4+) are frequently adopted. The aim of this preliminary study was to examine the association between the MCMI-III and the PDQ-4+ in a mixed Italian psychiatric sample.

All the correlations between the MCMI-III personality scales and the correspondent PDQ-4+ scales were positive and generally good. The only exceptions were represented by the Histrionic and Narcissistic PDs. Strong associations between several MCMI-III clinical scales and PDQ-4+ personality scales also emerged.

The present data support the good correspondence between the Italian versions of MCMI-III and PDQ-4+. Nevertheless, further research on the Histrionic and Narcissistic scales is necessary. Recent literature, however, seems to support our findings.

In: New Developments in Personality ...   ISBN: 978-1-62417-118-5
Editors: A. Morel and M. Durand   © 2013 Nova Science Publishers, Inc.

Chapter 1

GRANDIOSE AND VULNERABLE NARCISSISM: UNDERLYING DIMENSIONS AND CORRELATES

Jennifer M. Boldero, Richard C. Bell and Carol A. Hulbert
University of Melbourne, Australia

ABSTRACT

Narcissism is one of the oldest concepts in psychology, having its roots in Greek mythology and psychodynamic thought. It is studied in both clinical and social/personality psychology, with the clinical literature focusing on Narcissistic Personality Disorder (NPD) and the social/personality literature focusing on trait narcissism. It has been included in the Diagnostic and Statistical Manual of the Mental Disorders (DSM) since the third edition was published in 1980. Alongside clinical theory and research into NPD, research examining the correlates of trait narcissism continues to be popular. This distinguishes two narcissism forms, specifically grandiose (or overt) and vulnerable (or covert) narcissism. This distinction can be traced to the seminal psychodynamic work of Kernberg (1975), Kohut (1977), and Millon (1981). Grandiose narcissism is associated with exhibitionism, self-importance, and a preoccupation with receiving attention with others. Vulnerable narcissism is associated with hypersensitivity, anxiety, and insecurity although it is assumed that it is marked by unconscious feelings of grandeur which are proposed to be 'core' common to both forms (Wink, 1991). Grandiose narcissism is typically assessed using the 40-item Narcissistic Personality Inventory (NPI: Raskin & Hall, 1979) (NPI; Raskin & Hall, 1979), despite there being no consensus about its factor structure (e.g., Ackerman et al., 2011). Several measures of vulnerable narcissism exist, including the 52-item Pathological Narcissism Scale (PNI; Pincus et al., 2009), that assesses both grandiose and vulnerable narcissism, and the 10-item Hypersensitive Narcissism Inventory (HSNS), which is assumed to be uni-dimensional.

In this chapter, we first briefly review the nature of Narcissistic Personality Disorder (NPD) as considered in the various editions and revisions of the DSM. We then turn to the measurement of trait narcissism in social/personality psychology, discussing briefly criticisms of the NPI and considering the nature of the PNI and the HSNS. Following this discussion, we briefly present the results of our recent studies (Boldero & Bell, 2012a & b) that have established that the NPI assesses seven distinct correlated dimensions whereas the HSNS assesses two. Both the NPI and the HSNS factor structure is invariant across samples and the NPI factor structure is invariant when different question formats are used. Discussion then focuses on the interrelationships of these factors and their relationships with self-esteem. Following this, we consider this etiology, focusing on the propositions of Freud (1914/1957), Kernberg (1975), Kohut (1971, 1977), and Millon (1981). This highlights the role that interactions with caregivers likely play in the etiology of narcissism. Empirical evidence, obtained from two undergraduate samples, for the associations of the higher-order narcissism traits, and their lower-level dimensions, with recollections of cold and overvaluative parenting and with anxious and avoidant attachment is presented. We then turn to the role of self-regulation in narcissism, again considering the relationship of the higher-order traits narcissism traits, and their lower level dimensions, with self-regulatory factors, specifically, promotion, prevention, locomotion, and assessment. The chapter closes with the suggestion that research examining lower-level dimensions rather than the higher-level traits provides a better understanding of narcissism.

INTRODUCTION

The construct of narcissism was introduced into the psychological literature by Havelock Ellis in 1898. It was subsequently discussed by, among others, Rank (1914/1971), Freud (1914), and Murray (1938). This literature focused on narcissism as a personality characteristic or character disorder, with the term Narcissistic Personality Disorder (NPD) being first used by Kohut in 1968 (Levy, Ellison, & Reynoso, 2011). Many of the early theorists (e.g., Freud, 1914/1957; Kernberg, 1975; Kohut, 1971, 1977; Millon, 1981) proposed that narcissism develops in response to inadequate parenting.

Gunderson, Ronningstam, and Smith (1995) suggested that early discussions of narcissism resulted in the inclusion of NPD in the third edition of the DSM (DSM-III; American Psychiatric Association [APA], 1980). The disorder has remained in subsequent editions of the DSM and, despite a controversial proposal by the DSM-V working group to delete this personality disorder diagnostic category in the fifth edition and replace it by constellations of extreme trait ratings (Pincus, 2011), it has been announced that NPD will be retained.[1]

The DSM-IV task force found an NPD diagnosis is relatively unusual in both inpatient and outpatient settings (Gunderson et al., 1995). However, prevalence rates vary across settings. For example, Ronningstam (2009) reported the prevalence rate in clinical settings ranges from 1.3% to 17% and between 0% and 5.3% in the general population. Moreover, the disorder is more prevalent in males and younger adults (Miller & Campbell, 2010; Ronningstam, 2009).

As a result, few empirical investigations have compared individuals with NPD to those with other disorders (however, see, e.g., Ronningstam & Gunderson, 1990; Simonson & Simonson, 2011) and much of the literature focusing on NPD is either theoretical or presents case studies (Miller & Campbell, 2010).

This paucity of empirical clinical research can be contrasted to the "sizable body of research ... of narcissism as a "normal" trait" (Miller, Hoffman, Campbell, & Pilkonis, 2008, p. 141). This social/personality psychology research has "proved to be increasingly relevant and applicable to pathological narcissism" (Ronningstam, 2005, p. 289) because "much has been and will continue to be learned about narcissistic personality disorder through studies of narcissistic personality traits, even within college student samples" (Widiger, 2010, p. 193). Hence, this is the main focus in this chapter.

---

[1] See http://www.dsm5.org/proposedrevision/pages/personalitydisorders.aspx for the personality disorders to be included and other information about the DSM-V.

We first briefly review the nature of NPD, as defined in various revisions of the DSM. We do this to set the scene for considering recent discussions about the suitability of social/personality psychology measures in general, and the NPI and the HSNS in particular, as measures of "pathological" grandiose and vulnerable narcissism. This has occurred because some (e.g., Cain, Pincus, & Ansell, 2008; Miller & Campbell, 2008; Pincus et al., 2009; Pincus & Lukowitsky, 2010) have argued that the constructs are inconsistently defined and measured across the two disciplines.

We then consider the structure of the most commonly-used measure of narcissism, the Narcissistic Personality Inventory (NPI; Raskin & Hall, 1979), and two less commonly-used ones, the Pathological Narcissism Inventory (PNI; Pincus et al., 2009) and the Hypersensitive Narcissism Scale (HSNS; Hendin & Cheek, 1987).

These measures are assumed to assess the two forms discussed in both the clinical and social personality literature (e.g., Dickinson & Pincus, 2003; Hendin & Cheek, 1997; Rathvon & Holmstrom, 1996; Wink, 1991), specifically grandiose (or overt) narcissism and vulnerable (or covert) narcissism.

Despite being treated by the majority of researchers as uni-dimensional (i.e., they use scale scores as measures), evidence indicates that the NPI and the HSNS are multi-dimensional (e.g., Ackerman et al., 2011; Fossati et al., 2009; Huprich et al., 2012; Raskin & Terry, 1988).[2] We present further evidence of this multi-dimensionality from our recent work that also shows that the NPI and the HSNS factors load on a second-order factor (Boldero & Bell, 2012a & b).

We present evidence that is consistent with the proposition that there is a common 'core' to the two narcissism forms (e.g., Wink, 1991). Consideration of the associations between the NPI and HSNS factors with self-reported self-esteem, assessed using Rosenberg's (1965) self-esteem scale, allows examination of how this common 'core' is related to self-esteem, a factor that many, including Bosson and Weaver (2011), argue goes hand-in-hand with narcissism.

Finally, using data from two additional student samples, we examine the associations of our grandiose and vulnerable narcissism factors with the anxious and avoidant attachment and cold and overvaluative parenting dimensions which are implicated in the development of narcissism (e.g., Otway & Vignoles, 2006; Smolewska & Dion, 2005). We also examine the

---

[2] The PNI is multidimensional (Pincus et al., 2009).

associations with the self-regulatory factors of promotion, prevention, locomotion, and assessment that are necessary for self-regulatory success (Higgins, 1997; Higgins, Kruglanski, & Pierro, 2003; Kruglanski et al., 2000).

NPD IN THE DSM

As noted above, NPD as a diagnostic category was first included in the DSM-III. The eight criteria were a grandiose sense of one's own self-importance or uniqueness; a preoccupation with fantasies of unlimited success, power, brilliance, beauty, or ideal love; exhibitionism; responding to criticism, indifference, or defeat either with cool indifference or with marked feelings of rage, inferiority, shame, humiliation, or emptiness; a sense of entitlement; interpersonal exploitativeness; having relationships that vacillate between extremes of over-idealization and devaluation; and a lack of empathy (Cain et al., 2008; Raskin & Hall, 1979; 1981; Reynolds & Lejuez, 2011). When the DSM-III was revised in 1983, the vacillating relationships criterion was removed, criteria relating to entitlement and a preoccupation with feelings of envy added, and grandiosity and uniqueness became separate criteria (Cain et al., 2008; Reynolds & Lejuez, 2011).

The publication of the DSM-IV in 1994 saw grandiose features, including arrogance, haughty behaviors and/or attitudes, and beliefs that other people are envious of the individual added (Cain et al., 2008). The revised DSM-IV NPD criteria were: a grandiose sense of self-importance; a preoccupation with fantasies of unlimited power, success, brilliance, beauty, or ideal love; a belief that he/she is "special" or unique and can only be understood by, and should associate with, other special or high status people or institutions; requires excessive admiration; a sense of entitlement; interpersonal exploitativeness, a lack of empathy; often envious of others or believes that others are envious of him/her; and shows arrogant, haughty behaviors or attitudes (APA, 2000).[3]

The changes in NPD criteria from the DSM-III to the DSM-IV, thus, resulted in an emphasis on narcissistic grandiosity to the relative exclusion of narcissistic vulnerability (Cain et al., 2008).

---

[3] No revisions to NPD criteria were made in the DSM-IV-TR (Reynolds & Lejuez, 2011). Five of these nine criteria must be present for a diagnosis of NPD.

Although this conception of narcissism is consistent with lay understandings of the disorder (Buss & Chiodo, 1991), it is inconsistent with the clinical, psychiatric, and social/personality psychology literature that shows that narcissism involves vulnerability in addition to grandiosity (e.g., Cain et al., 2008; Dickinson & Pincus, 2003; Hendin & Cheek, 1997; Pincus & Lukowitsky, 2010; Rathvon & Holmstrom, 1996, Russ, Shedler, Bradley, & Westen, 2008; Wink, 1991).

Consistent with this distinction, Fossati et al. (2005) found that the DSM-IV NPD symptoms were best accounted for by two correlated factors. However, Miller et al. (2008) found that a one-, rather than a two-, factor model best accounted for these symptoms. In addition, when two factors were extracted, their correlations with scores on eight of nine PD scales (the exception was schizotypal PD), and anxiety and depression did not differ.

Miller et al. (2008) argued that sample and assessment differences between their study and that of Fossati et al. (2005) might account for the inconsistent results. They concluded that their results indicate that only one factor, which reflects narcissistic grandiosity, underlies the DSM-IV NPD symptoms. Further, they argued that this is consistent with clinicians' views of what the disorder is 'like' in terms of Big Five personality traits (e.g., Lynam & Widiger, 2001; Samuel & Widiger, 2004).

THE ASSESSMENT OF GRANDIOSE NARCISSISM IN SOCIAL/PERSONALITY PSYCHOLOGY RESEARCH

Social/personality psychology narcissism research was facilitated by the development of the NPI (Raskin & Hall, 1979). Not surprisingly, this scale is the most commonly-used measure of narcissism (del Rosario & White, 2005), with Cain et al. (2008) reporting that "since 1985, the NPI was used as the main or only measure of narcissistic traits in approximately 77% of social/personality research" (pp. 642-643). Indeed, a PsycINFO search including the phrase "narcissistic personality inventory" yields 715 peer-reviewed articles.[4]

When developing the NPI, Raskin and Hall (1979) specifically set out to measure the eight DSM-III NPD criteria. Although NPI scores are continuously rather than categorically distributed within the population (Foster & Campbell, 2007), they correlate as strongly, if not more strongly,

---

[4] Search conducted on 21 July, 2012.

with measures of NPD as any two measures of the disorder (Miller et al., 2009; Samuel & Widiger, 2008). For example, Maxwell, Donnellan, Hopwood, and Ackerman (2011) reported that the correlation between the NPI and the NPD items of the Personality Diagnostic Questionnaire-4 (PDQ-4; Hyler, 1994)[5] was .40.

In addition, Miller, Gaughan, Pryor, Kamen, and Campbell (2009) found that across a student and a clinical sample, NPI scores correlated .54 with scores on a semi-structured NPD interview.

Notwithstanding the frequent use of the NPI as a measure of grandiose narcissism and reliable finding of significant correlations with NPD scores, there has been an intense debate in the last few years about its use (Maxwell et al., 2011).

Criticisms include that it "does not assess subclinical narcissism, but rather predominantly assessed non-distressed adaptive expressions of narcissism" (Pincus & Lukowitsky, 2010, p. 425), that it focuses on grandiosity rather than vulnerability (e.g., Brown, Buzdek, & Tamborski, 2009; Cain et al., 2008), that its positive relationships with factors reflecting psychological health suggest that it is a measure of self-esteem rather than narcissism (Rosenthal & Hooley, 2010), and that it assesses two forms of narcissism as its component factors correlate differentially with different factors (Brown et al., 2009).[6] Miller and Campbell's (2011) cogent responses to these criticisms are now briefly considered.

First, the proposition that the NPI assesses a non-distressed form of narcissism (e.g., 'normal' narcissism) is based on results that indicate that NPI scores are negatively related to neuroticism, sadness, and depression, and positively related to extraversion, happiness, and self-esteem (e.g., Miller & Maples, 2011; Sedikides, Rudich, Gregg, Kumashiro, & Rusbult, 2004). However, NPI scores correlate with less adaptive factors (Twenge, Konrath, Foster, Campbell, & Bushman, 2008), including distorted judgments of one's ability (Paulhus, Harms, Bruce, & Lysy, 2003), risky decision-making (Campbell, Goodie, & Foster, 2004), and pathological gambling (Lakey, Rose, Campbell, & Goodie, 2008).

In addition, they correlate with Machiavellianism and psychopathy measures and these three factors are argued to constitute the 'dark triad'

---

[5] The PDQ-4 is a a self-report measure of personality disorder symptomotology.
[6] An additional concern is the lack of stability of the NPI's factor structure (e.g., Ackerman et al., 2011). We discuss this in the section of this chapter dealing with its factor structure.

(Miller et al., 2010; Paulhus & Williams, 2002).[7] These correlations with powerfully 'negative' factors led Miller and Foster (2011) to hope "that the field will refrain from referring to these NPI scores as *normal* or *nonpathological* narcissism, as there is nothing inherently normal or nonpathological about high scores on this scale" (p 150, italics in original).

Rosenthal and Hooley (2010) argued that NPI is confounded with self-esteem, containing items that assess this factor. They provided evidence that some NPI items assess less clearly narcissistic characteristics whereas other items assess more clearly narcissistic ones.

Scores on a scale using the more narcissistic items were more strongly related to NPD scores and were unrelated or negatively related to self-esteem than the less clearly narcissistic scale scores.[8] However, the central question is whether a grandiose narcissism measure should be strongly correlated with self-esteem.

Like Miller and Campbell (2011), we believe that it is difficult to conceptualize a valid self-report measure of grandiose narcissism that does not correlate with self-reported self-esteem.

Finally, there is the issue that the NPI assesses two forms of narcissism as its component factors correlate differentially with different factors. However, as Miller and Campbell (2011) noted, because the NPI is multidimensional, like all such constructs, its subscales have divergent relations with other factors.[9]

What is clear is that, when utilized as a uni-dimensional scale, the NPI assesses a construct that reflects grandiose narcissism and narcissism as defined by the DSM-IV. Furthermore, it accounts for incremental variance in personality traits considered to be important markers of NPD over and above other measures suggested as replacements for it (Miller, Price, & Campbell, 2012).

We now consider the two most commonly-used measures of vulnerable narcissism, the PNI (Pincus et al., 2009) and HSNS (Hendin & Cheek, 1997).[10]

---

[7] Recently, Schoenleber, Sadeh, and Verona (2011) found that scores on Ames, Rose, and Anderson's (2006) 16-item NPI version correlated with measures of manipulative and deceitful interpersonal style, and unprovoked aggression.

[8] See Rosenthal, Montoya, Ridings, Rieck, and Hooley (2011) for consistent results, but see Miller, Maples, and Campbell (2011b) for inconsistent ones.

[9] We return to this issue in our consideration of the correlates of the NPI factors in a subsequent section of this chapter.

[10] The PNI also measures grandiose narcissism.

THE ASSESSMENT OF VULNERABLE NARCISSISM: THE PNI AND THE HSNS

The PNI

The 52-item PNI was described by Pincus and Lutowisky (2010) as "the only multidimensional measure assessing clinically identified characteristics spanning the full phenotypic range of pathological narcissism" (p. 443). Its seven dimensions assess "problems with narcissistic grandiosity (Entitlement Rage, Exploitativeness, Grandiose Fantasy, Self-sacrificing Self-enhancement) and narcissistic vulnerability (Contingent Self-esteem, Hiding the Self, Devaluing)" (Pincus et al., 2009, p. 365). The scale was developed by subjecting 105 items to a principal components analysis (PCA)[11] and a reduced pool of 52 items to confirmatory factor analysis (CFA). However, Pincus et al. (2009) did not test whether their grandiosity and vulnerability factors loaded on second-order factor. Rather, they reported that the four grandiose subscales "had small positive correlations with the NPI" (p. 371)[12] whereas the three vulnerable subscales "had very small, often negative correlations with the NPI" (p. 371).

Wright, Lukowitsky, Pincus, and Conroy (2010) conducted three second-order CFAs of the PNI factors. In one all factors were specified to load on a single second-order factor. The remaining two analyses both tested whether the Grandiose fantasy (GR) and Exploitativeness (EX) factors loaded on the Grandiosity second-order factor and Contingent Self-esteem (CSE), Hiding the Self (HS), and Devaluating (DEV) factors loaded on the Vulnerability one. The difference between the two models was the factor which the Self-serving Self-enhancement (SSSE) and Entitlement Rage (ER) factors were specified to load on. The first model placed ER on the Grandiosity second-order factor and SSSE on the Vulnerability one. The second model placed SSSE on the Grandiosity second-order factor and ER on the Vulnerability one.

---

[11] As we argue below, based on the work of methodologists, PCA is not the most appropriate method to use when the latent constructs underlying a scale are of interest (see also Tamborski and Brown, 2011).

[12] The correlation between the NPI and the PNI Exploitative subscale was .56, which Cohen, (1988) suggested is large. This likely occurred because the five PNI items that define this scale are the narcissistic options of the five that define Raskin and Terry's (1987) Exploitativeness NPI component. Two other NPI narcissistic options are additional NPI items. These load on Raskin and Terry's (1988) entitlement scale. One of these loaded on Pincus et al.'s Grandiose fantasy factor and the other on their Entitlement/Rage factor.

All three CFAs yielded similar fit indices. However, the second two-factor model was selected on the basis of a slightly better fit according to the Akaike information criterion (AIC).[13] Wright et al. (2010) did not, however, test the fit of Pincus et al.'s (2009) structure (i.e., ER, EX, GR, and SSSE loading on the Grandiosity second-order factor and CSSE, HS, and DEV loading on the Vulnerability one). They reported that the correlation between the two second-order factors was .81 and that specifying the factors to correlate perfectly (i.e., a correlation of 1.0 and equivalent to a one-factor model) resulted in a poorer-fitting model.[14] Miller et al. (2011a) found that only two PNI factors, specifically EX and GF, loaded on their grandiose narcissism factor whereas the other five loaded on their vulnerable narcissism factor.[15] Finally, Zeigler-Hill and Besser (2011) found that Wright et al.'s (2010) grandiosity factor did not correlate with self-reported self-esteem. Taken together these results suggest that the PNI might not be the optimum measure of grandiose and vulnerable narcissism.

The HSNS

The 10-item HSNS was developed Hendin & Cheek (1997) who correlated Murray's (1938) 20-item Narcism Scale with a 35-item MMPI-based composite measure of narcissistic vulnerability (which they labelled covert narcissism). This measure comprised items from the Narcissistic Personality Disorder Scale (NPD; Ashby, 1978; Ashby, Lee, & Duke, 1979), the Narcissism-Hypersensitivity Scale (Serkownek, 1975), and the 40-item version of the NPI. Ten items from Murray's scale were selected for inclusion in the HSNS, primarily because they correlated positively with the MMPI measure and negatively with the NPI. Thus, not surprisingly, the NPI and the HSNS correlate, albeit weakly (e.g., Fossati et al., 2010; Hendin & Cheek, 1997; Luchner, Houston, Walker, & Houston, 2011). HSNS scores correlate negatively with self-esteem assessed using Rosenberg's (1965) self-esteem scale (e.g., Atlas & Them, 2008; Pincus et al., 2009). In addition, they correlate positively with Neuroticism and negatively with Extraversion and Agreeableness (Hendin & Cheek, 1987).

---

[13] This structure was also reported by Tritt, Ryder, Ring, & Pincus (2010) based on a PCA.

[14] Both Besser and Zeigler-Hill (2010, Study 1) and Zeigler-Hill and Besser (2011) reported correlations between the two PNI subscale scores of .61. However, Tritt et al. (2010) reported a correlation between their two components of only .16.

[15] Miller et al.'s (2011) EFA included Emmons (1984, 1987) four NPI factors and the HSNS.

THE FACTOR STRUCTURE OF THE NPI AND THE HSNS

The majority of studies using the NPI and the HSNS treat them as uni-dimensional scales. However, there is evidence that both scales are multi-dimensional.

The NPI

The NPI initially consisted of 80 item pairs, each comprising a narcissistic and a non-narcissistic statement, selected from a 223-item pool using item analysis (Raskin & Hall, 1979). The item pairs were divided into two forms that correlated substantially. However, Raskin and Hall (1981) reduced the number of items to 54. The NPI has a long history of being subjected to PCA and EFA. Emmons (1984) found that 37 of Raskin and Hall's (1981) 54 items had substantial loadings (i.e., > .35) on four principal components; a structure essentially replicated by Emmons (1987) using principal axis factoring. Raskin and Terry (1988) found that 40 items loaded on seven principal components whereas Kansai (2003) found 29 loaded on four that were similar to Emmons' (1987) factors. In contrast, Kubarych, Deary, and Austin (2004) found that two- and three-component models provided an adequate fit to 37 items whereas Corry, Merritt, Mrug, and Pamp (2008) decided that a two-factor solution was appropriate, with 23 items loading on these factors. Recently, Ackerman et al. (2011) found a three-factor solution for 25 items. They argued that these factors form two separate facets, one of which is positively associated with "adaptive" factors, such as self-esteem, and the other, made up of two factors, which is positively associated with some "adaptive" aspects (e.g., social potency) and some "socially toxic" ones (e.g., Machiavellanism). However, they did not formally evaluate whether these two factors load on a second-order one. Finally, Ames, Rose, and Anderson (2006) developed a brief 16-item version of the NPI. They reported that "loadings on the first unrotated factor ranged from .13 to .66 with the first factor capturing 19.9 percent of the variance" (p. 442). Taken together, the results of these studies indicate there is little agreement about the NPI's factor structure (e.g., Ackerman et al., 2011), which is problematic. One reason for the failure to replicate this structure is that researchers have not used the most optimal analytic techniques (Ackerman et al., 2011; Corry et al., 2008). There are three specific issues with the techniques used in these studies. First, the majority of researchers have used either Pearson's product moment correlation coefficients and/or PCA as the basis of the analyses. Because the NPI items are dichotomous forced-choice items, Pearson's correlation coefficients can give rise to spurious 'difficulty factors' (i.e., non-content based ones; Carroll, 1961; Lord & Novick, 1968) whereas tetrachoric correlations do not (Carroll, 1961; Muthén & Hofacker, 1988).

PCA yields summaries of observed variables as components, which can be conceived of as "the effects of rather than the causes of the variable correlations" (Reise, Waller, & Comrey, 2000, p. 294). In contrast, EFA yields latent variables that explain the variance (i.e., correlations) among items and, thus, a scale's latent structure (Costello & Osbourne, 2005; Fabrigar, Wegener, MacCallum, & Strahan, 1999; Tambowski & Brown, 2011). As a result, EFA based on tetrachoric correlations should be used to determine NPI's factor structure. Only Ackerman et al. (2011) used an EFA based on tetrachoric correlations.

The method used to decide the number of factors to extract is also an issue. Most studies examining the NPI's structure have used Cattell's (1966) scree plot, either alone or in combination with Kaiser's (1960) criterion of eigenvalues of greater than 1.0 (e.g., Ackerman et al., 2011; Corry et al., 2008; Emmons, 1984, 1987; Raskin & Terry, 1988). Both methods are unreliable (Crawford & Koopman, 1979; Reise et al., 2000; Streiner, 1998). Parallel analysis (Horn, 1965), which involves comparing eigenvalues extracted from data with that from random data, is the most reliable method. No NPI factor analytic studies have used parallel analysis to determine the number of factors to be extracted.[16]

Ideally, once the factor structure of a scale has been determined, subsequent studies should first use CFA to determine how well the established structure fits the data and then conduct EFA if the structure does not fit. However, until recently there were problems with CFA models (Marsh et al., 2010).

Specifically, the requirement that each item only load on one factor (i.e., an independent cluster model) was overly restrictive (Church & Burke, 1994) and often models did not fit the data.[17] It is likely that Corry et al. (2008)

---

[16] Corry et al. (2008) conducted a parallel analysis using both communality estimates but rejected the results on the basis of Steger's (2007) results and because the factors were not reliable. Ackerman et al. (2011) noted that this latter approach to determining the number of factors to extract can lead "to an underextraction of key factors" (p. 70).

[17] The finding of models that did not fit with earlier CFA models was common in personality research (Marsh et al., 2010)

used one of these models for their CFA of the NPI. New confirmatory models allow items to load on more than one factor (Marsh et al., 2010). One such model is that based on a combination of both exploratory and confirmatory techniques that can be estimated using Mplus (Muthén, & Muthén, 1988-2011).

In addition to these data analytic issues, the 'usual' NPI format could be problematic. The scale presents pairs of narcissistic and non-narcissistic statements to individuals who are asked to select the one that best describes them (i.e., it has a dichotomous forced-choice format). Raskin and Hall (1981) likely chose this format to overcome acquiescence bias problems. However, it is possible that for some individuals neither alternative is self-descriptive.

For example, an individual who does not tell stories as self-descriptive would have difficulty selecting between *Everybody likes to hear my stories* and *Sometimes I tell good stories.* Similarly, neither *I am going to be great person* nor *I hope I am going to be successful* would describe an individual who does not expect to be successful. This statement applicability problem possibly accounts for the low internal consistency estimates that have been reported for Raskin and Terry's (1988) NPI subscales (e.g., del Rosario & White, 2005).

Both Corry et al. (2008) and Kubarych et al. (2004) recognized this problem and suggested that the NPI item format be altered such that the narcissistic and non-narcissistic NPI statements are anchors for Likert scales. Although this format would facilitate factor analyses based on Pearson's correlation coefficients (which are easier to generate than tetrachoric correlations) and would allow "participants more freedom to express their traits" (Corry et al., 2008, p. 599), it does not overcome the problem of statement applicability. However, Barelds and Dijkstra (2010), Egan and McCorkindale (2007), and Egan and Lewis (2011) have used an NPI variant that presents the narcissistic statements of NPI items and asks participants to indicate the extent to which they agree that each statement describes them.

Barelds and Dijkstra (2010) found that scores on the Likert-scale variant correlated highly with those on Raskin and Terry's (1988) dichotomous forced-choice variant as did responses to individual items. They performed a PCA of the Likert-scale variant, extracting four and seven correlated factors. These solutions were rotated to target patterns of loadings reflecting Emmons' (1984) and Raskin and Terry's (1988) solutions.

Table 1. Loadings of NPI Items on the Seven-Factor Exploratory Factor Analysis Solution

Item	Narcissistic Statement	Factor[a]						
		1	2	3	4	5	6	7
7	I like to be the center of attention	.80						
30	I really like to be the center of attention	.79						
20	I will usually show off it I get the chance	.57						
2	Modesty doesn't become me	.49						
28	I like to start new fads and fashions	.39						
38	I get upset when people don't notice how I look when I go out in public	.35					.32	
37	I wish somebody would someday write my biography	.35						
3	I would do almost anything on a dare	.28				.26		
22	I rarely depend on anyone else to get things done		.76					
17	I like to take responsibility for making decisions		.62					
39	I am more capable than other people		.54					
21	I always know what I am doing		.43					
5	If I ruled the world it would be a better place		.28				.26	
19	I like to look at my body			.90				
29	I like to look at myself in the mirror			.86				
15	I like to show off my body			.78				
33	I would prefer to be a leader		.36		.64			
10	I see myself as a good leader				.64			
36	I am a born leader				.63			
32	People always seem to recognize my authority				.61			

Item	Narcissistic Statement	Factor[a]						
		1	2	3	4	5	6	7
1	I have a natural talent for influencing people				.57	.42		.30
11	I am assertive				.47			
12	I like having authority over other people		.30		.38		.26	
13	I find it easy to manipulate people					.86		
35	I can make anybody believe anything I want them to					.75		
6	I can usually talk my way out of anything					.66		
16	I can read people like a book					.40		
23	Everybody likes to hear my stories					.39		
25	I will never be satisfied until I get all that I deserve						.77	
24	I expect a good deal from other people						.68	
14	I insist on getting the respect that is due me						.55	
18	I want to amount to something in the eyes of the world						.52	
27	I have a strong will to power		.28				.37	
26	I like to be complimented						.33	
34	I am going to be a great person							.80
40	I am an extraordinary person							.76
9	I think I am a special person							.57
8	I will be a success				.29			.55
31	I can live my life anyway I want to		.30					.40
4	I know that I am good because everyone keeps telling me so							.35

From Boldero & Bell, 2012a. *Note:* Only loadings > .25 are shown.

[a] Because of their similarity to Raskin and Terry's (1987) components, Boldero and Bell (2012a) labelled the factors using Raskin and Terry's (1988) labels. Accordingly, Factor 1 is Exhibitionism, Factor 2 Self-Sufficiency, Factor 3 Vanity, Factor 4 Authority, Factor 5 Exploitativeness, Factor 6 Entitlement, and Factor 7 Superiority.

Congruence coefficients were used to determine similarities of the two sets of solutions. Neither solution was replicated although the fit of Raskin and Terry's (1988) model was better than that of Emmons (1984). Using data from two samples who completed either an NPI variant which either presented Likert scale items ($N = 545$) or dichotomous items ($N = 491$) that asked participants to indicate whether the narcissistic NPI statements were self-descriptive or not, we (Boldero & Bell, 2012a) examined whether these two variants had equivalent factor structures.[18] The versions can be thought of as measures of how self-descriptive the narcissistic items are and the number of items that are self-descriptive, which is consistent with the original scoring of the dichotomous forced-choice NPI scale. Using EFA (Sample 1) and CFA (Sample 2) based on tetrachoric correlations, the factor structure which best fit both variants essentially replicated Raskin and Terry's (1988) seven components (see Table 1). The seven factors were moderately correlated and had equivalent loadings on a second-order factor, indicating that the NPI assesses a higher-order factor identifiable as grandiose narcissism.

The HSNS

Although the HSNS was initially reported by Hendin and Cheek (1997) to be uni-dimensional, recent research suggests that it assesses two correlated factors. Fossati et al. (2009) conducted separate PCAs of data from a clinical and a non-clinical sample using an Italian translation of the HSNS. The two correlated components extracted separately for each sample were labeled Oversensitivity to Judgment and Egocentrism.

Six items had substantial loadings (i.e., > .30) on the Oversensitivity to Judgment component whereas four had substantial loadings on the Egocentrism one (see Table 2). Egocentrism was weakly positively correlated with the NPI for both samples whereas Oversensitivity to Judgment was not. Huprich, Luchner, Roberts, and Poulit (2012) conducted a combined EFA of the HSNS and the Depressive Personality Disorder Inventory (DPDI; Huprich, Margrett, Barthelemy, & Fine, 1996). Using a parallel analyses (Horn, 1965), they extracted six factors.

---

[18] We also tested the fit of all models reported in the literature using CFA. No model fitted although Raskin and Terry's (1987) PCA model was the best fit.

Table 2. Standardized factor loadings found in the exploratory factor analysis

Item	Factor 1	Factor 2[e]
I can become entirely absorbed in thinking about my personal affairs, my health, my cares or my relations to others[ac]	.36	
My feelings are easily hurt by ridicule or by the slight remarks of others[ac]	.76	
When I enter a room I often become self-conscious and feel that the eyes of others are upon me[ad]	.48	
I dislike sharing the credit of an achievement with others[bd]		.42
I dislike being with a group unless I know that I am appreciated by at least one of those present[ac]	.30	
I feel that I am temperamentally different from most people[ad]		.30
I often interpret the remarks of others in a personal way[ac]	.72	
I easily become wrapped up in my own interests and forget the existence of others[bd]		.55
I feel that I have enough on my hands without worrying about other people's troubles[bd]		.74
I am secretly "put out" when other people come to me with their troubles, asking for my time and sympathy[bd]		.59

From Boldero & Bell, 2012b. *Note*: Only loadings >.25 are shown.

[a] Items found by Fossati et al. (2009) to load on the Oversensitivity to Judgment component.
[b] Items found by Fossati et al. (2009) to load on the Egocentrism component.
[c] Item found by Huprich et al. (2012) to load on the Hypersensitive Self-focus factor.
[d] Item found by Huprich et al. (2012) to load on the Narcissistic Self-focus factor.
[e] Boldero and Bell (2012) labeled Factor 1 Hypersensitivity and Factor 2 Narcissistic self-focus.

Nine HSNS items had significant loadings on one of two factors which they labeled Hypersensitive Self-focus and Narcissistic Self-focus.[19] The remaining items had cross loadings on Hypersensitive Self-focus and a DPDI factor.

Fossati et al.'s (2009) and Huprich et al.'s (2012) models are similar. Five items that loaded on Fossati et al.'s (2009) Oversensitivity to Judgment component also loaded on Huprich et al.'s (2012) Hypersensitive Self-focus factor. Similarly, four items that loaded on Fossati et al.'s (2009) Egocentrism scale also loaded on Huprich et al.'s (2012) Narcissistic Self-focus factor. However, the item *I am temperamentally different from other people* loaded on Fossati et al.'s (2009) Hypersensitive Self-focus component and on Huprich et al.'s (2012) Narcissistic Self-focus factor. These differences in results likely arose because Huprich et al. (2012) analyzed the HSNS jointly with the DPDI and/or Fossati et al. (2009) used a PCA.

Using data from two samples ($N = 693$ & $N = 419$)[20], we found that a two-factor model best fit the HSNS data for both samples (Boldero & Bell, 2012b). The pattern of factor loadings was more similar to that of Huprich et al. (2012) than to Fossati et al. (2009) (see Table 2). We also found that the two factors were nested under a higher-order factor, indicating that, along with assessing two lower-order factors, the HSNS also assesses a higher-order one identifiable as vulnerable narcissism.

CORRELATIONS BETWEEN THE NPI AND HSNS FACTORS

Using the data from our second sample (i.e., that which completed the dichotomous NPI version), we examined the correlations between the NPI second-order factor and the two HSNS factors (Boldero & Bell, 2012b). These correlations were of interest for two reasons. First, previous studies that have used both the NPI and the HSNS have reported that they are, at best, weakly positively correlated (e.g., Fossati et al., 2009; Hendin & Cheek, 1997; Luchner et al., 2011). Although, this weak correlation is consistent with the proposition that both narcissism forms share a common 'core' (e.g., Wink, 1991), it does not provide any information about what this 'core' might be. Correlating our factors provided this information.

---

[19] Huprich et al. (2012) conducted their analyses using Mplus (Muthén & Muthén, 1988-2011) which determines the significance of factor loadings.

[20] The second sample is that which Boldero and Bell (2012a) used to examine the factor structure of the dichotomous version of the NPI.

Previous studies have found that HSNS scores are positively correlated with Raskin and Terry's (1988) Entitlement factor (Hendin & Cheek, 1997) and with Emmons' (1987) Entitlement/Exploitativeness one (Ryan, Weikel, & Sprechini, 2008). Indeed, Emmons' (1987) factor has been used as measures of vulnerable narcissism (e.g., Bosson & Prewitt-Freilino, 2007). The second-order NPI factor correlated negatively with the HSNS Hypersensitivity factor and positively with the Narcissistic Self-focus one, indicating that a narcissistic self-focus is common to both grandiose and vulnerable narcissism. This result also suggests that simply correlating HSNS and NPI scores masks the differential nature of these relationships.

Further examination of the narcissistic self-focus elements was provided by the correlations of the NPI and the HSNS factors. Both HSNS factors correlated positively with NPI Entitlement. Furthermore, they both correlated negatively with NPI Exhibitionism whereas neither correlated with NPI Superiority.

Although there were other associations between other HSNS and NPI factors (i.e., HSNS Narcissistic Self-focus correlated positively with NPI Self-sufficiency, Vanity, and Entitlement; HSNS Hypersensitivity correlated negatively with NPI Vanity and Authority), it appears that entitlement is a core feature of both grandiose and vulnerable narcissism and that exhibitionism differentiates between them.

Miller et al. (2011a) also found evidence that entitlement might be common to the two narcissism forms. Both grandiose and vulnerable narcissism factor scores, obtained from a principal factor axis of the NPI and PNI scales along with the HSNS,[21] were correlated with scores on Campbell, Bonacci, Shelton, Exline, and Bushman's (2004) Psychological Entitlement Scale.

These results are partially consistent with those studies that have found that the HSNS correlates positively with Emmons' (1987) NPI Entitlement/Exploitativeness factor (Hendin & Cheek, 1997; Ryan et al., 2008) and with Corry et al.'s (2008) Exhibitionism/Entitlement one (Miller et al., 2011a). However, they indicate that consideration of the dimensions of both scales allows for a more nuanced understanding of the relationships between grandiose and vulnerable narcissism.

---

[21] The grandiose factor had loadings from Corry et al.'s (2008) Leadership/Authority and Exhibitionism/Entitlement factors and Pincus et al.'s (2009) Exhibitionism and Grandiose fantasies factors. The vulnerable factor had loadings from Pincus et al.'s (2009) Contingent self-esteem, Self-sacrificing Self-enhancement, Grandiose fantasy, Hiding the self, Devaluing the self, and Entitlement-Rage factors along with the HSNS.

RELATIONS OF THE NPI AND THE HSNS FACTORS WITH SELF-ESTEEM

One of the central features of narcissism is self-aggrandizement and self-enhancement (e.g., Brown & Zeigler-Hill, 2004; Campbell, Reeder, Sedikides, & Elliot, 2000). Indeed, Morf and Rhodewalt's (2001) dynamic self-regulatory model proposes that one of the key features of narcissism is the struggle to maintain a grandiose yet fragile self-image. They proposed that narcissists use a range of strategies designed to allow the maintenance of a self that is extraordinary and superior to others, including self-enhancement. Propositions, such as this, have led researchers to examining the associations between self-reported self-esteem and narcissism (e.g., Brown & Bosson, 2001; Dickinson & Pincus, 2003; Rose, 2002).[22]

As noted above, the NPI correlates positively with self-esteem, although the strength of the correlations depends on how self-esteem is assessed. Brown and Zeigler-Hill (2004) found stronger correlations with self-esteem measures to the extent that the measure correlates with dominance. Thus, the Self-attributes Questionnaire (Pelham & Swann, 1989) and the Texas Social Behavior Inventory (Helmreich, Stapp, & Ervin, 1974) correlated more strongly with the NPI than Rosenberg's (1965) self-esteem scale (RSES). Despite this, most studies that have examined the associations of grandiose and vulnerable narcissism with self-esteem have used the RSES. These studies have found, not surprisingly, that NPI scores correlate positively with the RSES whereas HSNS scores correlate negatively (e.g., Atlas & Them, 2008; Brown & Zeigler-Hill, 2004; Rose, 2002; Sedikides et al., 2004).

Again using the data from our second sample (i.e., those who completed the dichotomous NPI version), we were able to examine the correlations of the two HSNS and seven NPI factors with self-esteem, assessed using the RSES (Boldero & Bell, 2012b). When doing this, we were mindful that the RSES has a bi-factor structure such that all items load on a global self-esteem factor and on one or two 'method' factors (DiStefano & Motl, 2006, 2009; Halama, 2008). These method factors have loadings on the positively- and negatively-worded RSES items, respectively, which, when not accounted for bias the self-esteem estimate. Accordingly, we conducted an EFA of the RSES and used factor scores on the global self-esteem factor, thus ensuring that we were using a relatively 'pure' self-esteem estimate.

---

[22] As noted above, Miller and Campbell (2011) also argued that any measure of grandiose narcissism should be correlated with self-reported self-esteem.

Both HSNS factors were negatively correlated with the global self-esteem factor (Hypersensitivity, $r = -.30$, $p < .001$; Narcissistic self-focus, $r = -.23$, $p < .001$). In addition, NPI Entitlement, which our analysis suggested is the 'core' of these two narcissism forms, was negatively related to the global self-esteem factor, $r = -.15$, $p = .03$. Of the other NPI factors, Exhibitionism, Vanity, Authority, and Superiority were positively related to self-esteem (rs between .53 and .21, all ps $< .001$) whereas Self-sufficiency and Exploitativeness were unrelated. These findings are consistent with the notion that entitlement serves to protect the individual against information that reflects a negative self-view.

THE ETIOLOGY OF NARCISSISM

A number of clinical theorists have discussed the etiology of grandiose and vulnerable narcissism. The basic premise of these discussions is that parents 'teach' their children to be narcissistic by altering the normal progression from childhood narcissism to adult relating (Horton, 2011). Here we discuss briefly four perspectives, specifically, those of Freud (1914/1957), Kernberg (1975), Kohut (1971, 1977), and Millon (1981) as these are most frequently discussed in the empirical literature (e.g., Otway & Vignoles, 2006).

Of the psychoanalytic theorists, Freud (1914/1957), in his seminal essay *On Narcissism*, argued that narcissism is a normal part of development. However, later in development, rather than directing their love outwards (as is the case for anaclitic individuals who initially direct love to parents and later to others), those who are narcissistic direct their love inwards. This direction of love to the self rather than to others can either be a result of parental love or parental rejection.

Both Kernberg (1975) and Kohut (1971, 1977), like Freud (1914/1957), conceptualized narcissism as a normal aspect of development. However, they argued that the disorder occurs when parenting is inadequate, resulting in an ability to maintain self-cohesion and realistic self-esteem.

Kernberg (1975) focused predominantly on grandiose narcissism, discussing how narcissists libidinally invest in a sense of self that is based on immature real and ideal self-representations. This occurs when parents are strict, unloving, or hostile. In this case, children have no ideal object (i.e., the parent) to internalize and they are unable to form a stable core of self-regard (i.e., self-esteem). Kernberg (1975) also argued that often those who become narcissistic were 'special' in that they were regarded as "the only 'brilliant' child or the one who is supposed to fulfill family aspirations" (p. 235). Thus, according to Kernberg (1975), both overvaluative and cold/rejecting parenting can lead to narcissism.

Kohut (1971, 1977) addressed the etiology of both forms of narcissism. He proposed that if parents engage in empathic mirroring, grandiose exhibitionism is fostered whereas when parents are role models for their children for children's behavior, idealization occurs.

These dimensions develop when parents are supportive but the child is left to their own 'devices' (i.e., without guidance and parental affirmation) from time to time. He proposed that when this does not occur, horizontal or vertical splitting can occur, leading to the development of grandiose or vulnerable narcissism, respectively.

Finally, Millon (1981, 1996) proposed that his five narcissistic sub-types develop from a blend of personality styles which are a result of excessive parental indulgence and admiration. This type of parenting leads children to develop expectations that others will treat them in a manner similar to their parents and they come to believe that others are beneath them, weak, and easily manipulated.

Together, these propositions have led to the consideration of the associations of both narcissism forms with recollections of parents as warm or overvaluing or as cold and rejecting (e.g., Otway & Vignoles, 2009). Alongside this interest in parenting, researchers have considered associations between the two narcissism forms and the attachment dimensions of anxiety and avoidance.

This research is based on Bowlby's (1988) proposition that early experiences with caregivers affect adult personality through internal working models of what the individual, others, and the world are 'like' (i.e., internal working models).

These internal working models are the basis of attachment. Meyer and Pilkonis (2005, see also Meyer & Pilkonis, 2011) proposed that, of Ainsworth, Blehar, Waters, and Wall's (1978) three attachment types, individuals with NPD would be dismissive or fearful. Furthermore, those with overindulgent parents would be more likely to be dismissive whereas those with cold or rejecting parents would be more likely to be fearful. Consistent with this proposition, cold parenting is associated with an avoidant attachment style whereas warm and uncritical parenting is associated with a secure rather than anxious attachment style (Hazan & Shaver, 1987).

NARCISSISM, PARENTING AND ATTACHMENT

Dickinson and Pincus (2003) found, consistent with the proposition that parenting is associated with narcissism, that those classified as grandiose narcissists report a secure or dismissive attachment style on the Adult Attachment Questionnaire (Batholomew & Horowitz, 1991) whereas those classified as vulnerable narcissists report a fearful or preoccupied attachment style. Similarly, NPI scores are positively correlated with reports of parental warmth (Horton, Bleau, & Drweci, 2006). However, Otway and Vignoles (2006) found that their two latent factors, labeled overt and covert narcissism (indicated by three-item parcels of NPI and HSNS items, respectively), were positively associated with recollections of both parental coldness and overvaluation in a structural equation model in which both narcissism forms were modeled simultaneously.[23] They also included in their analyses the attachment dimensions of anxiety and avoidance, assessed using the Experiences in Close Relationships Scale (ECR; Brennan, Clark, & Shaver, 1998). Anxious attachment was positively related to the covert narcissism but not to overt narcissism. In addition, avoidant attachment was unrelated to either latent factor.

Using a canonical correlational analysis, Smolewska and Dion (2005) found that anxious attachment was positively associated with HSNS scores but not those on the NPI. Avoidant attachment was also positively associated with the HSNS, albeit not as strongly as anxious attachment. The difference between these results and those of Otway and Vignoles (2006) likely reflects the specific data analytic techniques used and the variables included in the analyses.

Otway and Vignoles (2006) also investigated the associations between recollections of parental coldness and overvaluation and scores on Raskin and Terry's (1988) seven NPI subscales using structural equation models. Parental coldness and overvaluation were both positively associated with authority and exhibitionism whereas overvaluation alone was positively associated with entitlement and superiority. Neither factor was associated with exploitativeness, self-sufficiency, or vanity. However, they did not include the attachment dimensions or the HSNS in these analyses.

Finally, Miller et al. (2011) examined the associations between anxious and avoidant attachment, assessed using the Experiences in Close Relationships – Revised Scale (ECR-R; Fraley, Waller, & Brennan, 2000)

---

[23] Otway and Vignoles (2006) included both latent factors to account for their covariation.

and grandiose and vulnerable narcissism factor scores. Consistent with Smolewska and Dion's (2005), but inconsistent with Otway and Vignoles' (2006) results, the vulnerable narcissism factor scores were positively correlated with both attachment dimensions, with anxiety being more strongly associated than avoidance.

We were able to use data from two new samples (Sample 1, $N = 185$; Sample 2, $N = 193$) to essentially replicate Otway and Vignoles' (2006) and Smolewska and Dion's (2005) studies. Sample 1 participants completed Boldero and Bell's (2012a) dichotomous NPI version whereas Sample 2 participants completed the Likert-scale version. Both samples also completed the ECR (Brennan et al., 1998) and Sample 2 participants completed Otway and Vignoles' (2006) recollections of parental overvaluation and coldness. Like Otway and Vignoles (2006), we used structural equation modeling, conducted in Mplus 6.0 (Muthén & Muthén, 1988-2011), in which the two forms were modeling simultaneously to account any covariation between them (Sample 1, $r = .09$, $p = .196$; Sample 2, $r = .22$, $p = .017$). However, rather than using NPI and HSNS scores or item parcels as indicators of the latent factors, we used scores on the seven NPI and on the two HSNS factors as indicators of the two narcissism forms. Conducting the analysis in Mplus allowed us to use Bayesian estimation which is preferable to traditional approaches (i.e., frequentist ones) for a number of reasons (see Boldero & Bell, 2012c). Before conducting the analyses, we examined the internal consistency of the scales that assessed seven NPI and two HSNS factors. For both samples the HSNS scales had adequate internal consistency.[24] In addition, the Likert scale NPI version scales were internally consistent. However, three of the seven NPI scales, assessed using the dichotomous version, were not.[25] Thus, the results for Sample 1 need to be interpreted with caution. When only anxious and avoidant attachment were included in the analysis, consistent with both Smolewska and Dion's (2005) and Otway and Vignoles' (2006) results, neither attachment dimension predicted grandiose narcissism for both samples (see Table 3). However, inconsistent with Smolewska and Dion's (2005) results, but consistent with those of Otway and Vignoles (2006), both anxious and avoidant attachment were predictors vulnerable narcissism, with avoidant attachment being a stronger predictor of this type of narcissism than anxious attachment.

---

[24] Adequate internal consistency was assumed when Cronbach's (1951) alpha was > .60.
[25] The scales that were not internally consistent were Self-Sufficiency, Entitlement, and Superiority.

Table 3. Results of the Path Analyses predicting NPI and HSNS factors from Anxious and Avoidant Attachment

Factor	Sample 1				Sample 2	
	Anxious	Avoidant		Anxious		Avoidant
Grandiose narcissism	.01	.09		.05		-.01
Vulnerable narcissism	.25**	.52***		.22**		.53***
NPI Exhibitionism	.03	.09		-.03		-.01
NPI Self-sufficiency	.08	.01		.01		.14***
NPI Vanity	.17*	.06		.03		-.01
NPI Authority	.09	.03		.03		-.05
NPI Exploitativeness	.02	.02		-.01		-.08
NPI Entitlement	.07	.05		-.02		-.01
NPI Superiority	.18*	-.08		.01		-.16
NPI Hypersensitivity	.14**	.42***		.48***		.08
NPI Narcissistic Self-focus	.24**	.38***		.35***		.24***

*$p < .05$; **$p < .01$; ***$p < .001$.
Note: Beta weights are shown.

We were able to include Otway and Vignoles' (2006) recollections of parenting dimensions in the analysis for our second sample. Again, consistent with their results, neither attachment dimension predicted grandiose narcissism whereas both predicted vulnerable narcissism (anxious, β = .45, p < .001; avoidant, β = .17, p = .037). However, the finding that only recollections of overvaluative parenting, β = .20, p < .001, predicted grandiose narcissism was inconsistent with their findings. Furthermore, neither parenting dimension was a predictor of vulnerable narcissism.

We examined the predictors of the NPI and HSNS factors from the attachment dimensions for both samples and jointly with recollections of parenting factors using the data from our second sample. The attachment dimensions were included because the HSNS factors were in these analyses.

When the attachment dimensions alone were considered as predictors, both predicted the two HSNS factors for Sample 1. However, for Sample 2, only anxious attachment predicted HSNS Hypersensitivity. Neither dimension predicted NPI Exhibitionism, Self-sufficiency, Authority, Exploitativeness, or Entitlement for Sample 1. Avoidant attachment predicted NPI Vanity and Superiority. Similarly, for Sample 2 neither dimension predicted NPI Exhibitionism, Authority, Exploitativeness, or Entitlement, but avoidant attachment predicted Superiority. Finally, anxious attachment predicted NPI Self-sufficiency whereas neither dimension predicted NPI Vanity.

These differences in results likely reflect the different nature of our two NPI variants including their internal consistencies. As noted above, Sample 1 participants indicated whether or not the grandiose characteristics were or were not self-descriptive of them whereas Sample 2 participants indicated the extent to which the characteristics were self-descriptive. This latter scale appears to provide a more sensitive index of the self-descriptiveness of these characteristics, and one which allowed more intuitive relationships to be revealed. For example, it is not surprising that those higher in avoidant attachment report being more self-sufficient whereas there is no reason to assume that those higher in anxious attachment would report being more vain. Similarly, there is no reason to assume that those higher in avoidant attachment would report being more hypersensitive whereas the relationship with anxious attachment is entirely understandable. Finally, the positive relationships of anxious and avoidant attachment with the HSNS Narcissistic self-focus factor is not surprising. The items with high loadings on this factor refer to feelings that individuals high in avoidance (e.g., *I feel I have enough on my hands without worrying about other people's troubles*) and anxiety (e.g., *I am secretly "put out" when other people come to me with their troubles, asking for my time and sympathy*) might experience.

Finally, when we included recollections of overvaluative and cold parenting in the analysis of Study 2 data, consistent with Otway and Vignoles' (2006) results, both overvaluative, $\beta = .28$, $p < .001$, and cold parenting recollections, $\beta = .23$, $p < .001$, were positively associated with Exhibitionism. However, inconsistent with their results, only overvaluation, $\beta = .20$, $p < .001$, was positively associated with Authority. Also inconsistent was the finding that both types of recollection were positively associated with Self-sufficiency (overvaluative, $\beta = .21$, $p < .001$; cold, $\beta = .16$, $p = .010$), Exploitativeness (overvaluative, $\beta = .31$, $p < .001$; cold, $\beta = .14$, $p = .020$), Entitlement (overvaluative, $\beta = .27$, $p < .001$; cold, $\beta = .16$, $p = .010$), and Superiority (overvaluative, $\beta = .29$, $p < .001$; cold, $\beta = .16$, $p = .010$). Neither type of recollection predicted HSNS Hypersensitivity. In contrast, the Narcissistic Self-focus factor was positively associated with cold parenting recollections, $\beta = .12$, $p = .020$).

Consistent with the results of the analysis in which only the attachment dimensions were considered as predictors, neither attachment dimension predicted NPI Exhibitionism, Vanity, Authority, Exploitativeness, or Entitlement. However, anxious, $\beta = .15$, $p = .040$, rather than avoidant attachment, was positively associated with Self-sufficiency. Similarly, avoidant attachment, $\beta = -.15$, $p = .040$, but not anxious attachment, was negatively associated with Superiority. Finally, consistent with the results of the previous analysis, HSNS Hypersensitivity was positively associated with only anxious attachment, $\beta = .49$, $p < .001$, whereas both attachment dimensions and cold parenting recollections were positively associated with the Narcissistic self-focus factor (avoidant attachment, $\beta = .21$, $p < .001$; anxious attachment, $\beta = .33$, $p < .001$; cold, $\beta = .12$, $p = .020$).

These differing patterns of relationships across analyses occurred because of the inclusion of parenting recollections. They suggest that suppression effects occurred when we considered the attachment dimensions as predictors of our seven grandiose narcissism dimensions on their own. Removing the variance shared by cold parenting recollections with both avoidant and anxious attachment ($r = .25$, $p < .001$; $r = .24$, $p < .001$, respectively) changed the pattern of relationships for Self-sufficiency and Superiority. Reporting being more self-sufficient was positively related to anxious attachment, possibly because of fears of rejection when asking for help. Similarly, reporting being more superior was positively related to avoidant attachment, possibly because not confiding in romantic partners or relying on them promotes superiority. It is also possible that the changed pattern of covariation of the scales, which resulted from using the NPI variants, also influenced the nature of these relationships.

SELF-REGULATION AND NARCISSISM

Self-aggrandizement and entitlement are central features of grandiose narcissism. According to Morf and Rhodewalt (2001), these are a result of a dynamic self-regulatory system that serves to maintain or increase self-esteem. They proposed that individuals engage in motivated self-construction efforts that result in short-term gains at the expense of long-term losses, particularly in the social arena. These efforts are argued to occur because these individuals' grandiose self-views are fragile and underpinned by deep-seated feelings of inferiority. Likewise, vulnerable narcissism has been proposed to occur when individuals' personal outcomes fall short of their grandiose expectancies (Bosson & Prewitt-Freilino, 2007). Thus, these individuals manifest low self-reported self-esteem underpinned by grandiose feelings which they are too insecure to act on (e.g., Dickinson & Pincus, 2003).

These propositions have resulted in research examining whether NPI scores are associated with high self-reported self-esteem in the presence of low implicit self-esteem and whether HSNS scores are associated with low self-reported self-esteem in the presence of high implicit self-esteem.[26] Implicit self-esteem is assessed using techniques, such as the Implicit Association Test (IAT; Greenwald, McGee, & Schwartz, 1998) or the Name Letter Task (NLT; Kitayama & Karasawa, 1997), that are assumed to assess individual's automatic responses and circumvent efforts to control impressions (Bosson et al., 2008). Although initial research was supportive of this proposition for overt narcissism (Jordan, Spencer, Zanna, Hoshino-Browne, & Correll, 2003; Zeigler-Hill, 2006) and covert narcissism (Bosson & Prewitt-Freilino, 2007), a review of research findings challenged this view (Bosson et al., 2008). This may, of course, reflect the unreliability of, and other problems with, implicit self-esteem measures (e.g., Bosson, Swann, & Pennebaker, 2000; Buhrmester, Blanton, & Swann, 2011; Krizan, 2008).

---

[26] This has been termed the mask model of narcissism. See also Gregg and Sedikides (2010) for a different perspective on the relationships of narcissism with implicit and explicit self-esteem.

What remains is that NPI scores are positively related to self-reported self-esteem whereas HSNS scores are negatively related (e.g., Atlas & Them, 2008; Pincus et al., 2009). However these results do not shed any light on the processes underlying narcissistic self-regulation. Campbell and associates' (e.g., Campbell, Brunell, & Finkel, 2006; Campbell & Foster, 2007) agency model of narcissism proposes that, because narcissistic individuals are unconditionally rewarded and overprotected from failure during childhood, they learn that their behavior will be rewarded and not punished and become focused on attaining positive outcomes but not on preventing negative ones.

Using the agency model, Foster and Trimm (2008) argued that NPI scores should be positively associated with approach motivation and negatively associated with avoidance motivation and that covert narcissism, assessed using three measures,[27] should be positively associated with avoidance motivation (they made no predictions about the associations of covert narcissism and approach motivation). In three studies, their predictions concerning NPI scores were confirmed and approach and avoidance motivation fully mediated the positive association between these scores and self-esteem. Further, in one study covert narcissism was positively related to avoidance motivation but this factor only partially mediated the negative association of this narcissism type and self-esteem. No relationships were found with approach motivation.

While these results are illuminating, they do not provide evidence that being focused on attaining positive outcomes is implicated in the etiology of grandiose narcissism whereas being more focused on preventing negative outcomes is implicated in the etiology of vulnerable narcissism. A rigorous investigation of these relationships requires modeling grandiose and vulnerable narcissism as the dependent variables in an analysis with factors that reflect a concern with being sensitive to the presence or absence of positive outcomes and with being sensitive to the absence or presence of negative outcomes. These factors are Higgins' (1997) promotion and prevention concerns.

Promotion and prevention concerns are proposed to arise in experiences with caregivers (Higgins & Silberman, 1998) and reflect different orientations toward attaining or maintaining desired end-states. Individuals with promotion concerns are sensitive to gains and the presence of positive outcomes (Higgins, 1997). Consequently, they prefer using eager goal pursuit

---

[27] The measures used were the HSNS, the NPD (Ashby, 1978; Ashby, Lee, & Duke, 1979), and Serkownek's (1975) Narcissism Scale.

means (e.g., Liberman, Idson, Camancho, & Higgins, 1999), consider multiple hypotheses (e.g., Friedman & Förster, 2001), and are generally more disposed toward taking chances (e.g., Zhou & Pham, 2004). By contrast, those with prevention concerns are sensitive to non-loss and the absence of negative outcomes (Higgins, 1997). Consequently, they prefer using vigilance goal pursuit means (e.g., Liberman et al., 1999), consider fewer alternatives (e.g., Friedman & Förster, 2001), and are generally more conservative (e.g., Zhou & Pham, 2004).

These concerns are operationalized as individuals' subjective histories of being successful at either attaining positive outcomes (promotion) and at preventing negative outcomes (prevention) using the Regulatory Focus Questionnaire (RFQ; Higgins et al., 2001). Both promotion and prevention success are negatively associated with depression, anxiety, interpersonal sensitivity, and obsessive compulsive disorder features (Grant & Higgins, 2003). Based on Foster and Trimm's (2008) results, promotion should be positively associated with grandiose narcissism whereas prevention should be positively associated with vulnerable narcissism. In addition, it is likely that promotion is negatively associated with vulnerable narcissism whereas prevention is negatively associated with grandiose narcissism.

Alongside promotion and prevention, self-regulation involves two processes, locomotion and assessment (Higgins et al., 2003; Kruglanski, Orehek, Higgins, Pierro, & Shalev, 2010).

Locomotion involves the movement from state to state and is positively associated with prompt action, staying focused on tasks, and goal pursuit striving (Kruglanski et al., 2000). By contrast, assessment reflects making comparisons and critically evaluating alternatives and other people. Locomotion is negatively associated with reporting more borderline personality disorder symptoms whereas assessment is positively associated with these reports (Bornovaloa, Fishman, Strong, Kruglanski, & Lejuez, 2008).

Similarly, locomotion is positively associated with self-esteem whereas assessment is negatively related (Kruglanski et al., 2000). Individuals' tendencies to focus on locomotion and assessment, like promotion and prevention, arise from experiences with caregivers (Kruglanski et al., 2000).

Locomotion and assessment, assessed using the Regulatory Mode Questionnaire (RMQ; Kruglanski et al., 2000), are, at best, weakly correlated. As self-aggrandizement and self-esteem are characteristics of grandiose narcissism as is criticism of others (Watson, Trumpeter, & O'Leary, 2006), we predicted that locomotion and assessment would be predictors of this narcissism form. However, as vulnerable narcissism is negatively associated with self-esteem and is also likely associated with criticism of others, we predicted that locomotion would likely be negatively associated with this form whereas assessment would be positively associated. As both our samples completed the RFQ and the RMQ, we were able to examine the predictors of our grandiose and vulnerable narcissism latent factors and of our seven NPI and two HSNS factors.

For Sample 1, consistent with our predictions, both grandiose and vulnerable narcissism were positively associated with assessment (see Table 4). Further, grandiose narcissism was positively associated with locomotion whereas vulnerable narcissism was negatively associated. However, inconsistent with predictions, grandiose narcissism was unrelated to promotion and vulnerable narcissism was unrelated to prevention. Moreover, vulnerable narcissism and promotion were positively associated. In contrast, for Sample 2, consistent with predictions, grandiose narcissism was positively associated with promotion and assessment and negatively associated with prevention.

In addition, vulnerable narcissism was negatively associated with promotion and locomotion and positively associated with assessment. Finally, inconsistent with predictions, locomotion was unrelated to grandiose narcissism and vulnerable narcissism was unrelated to prevention.

Relationships of our self-regulation factors with NPI and HSNS factors were relatively complex. For Sample 1, prevention was unrelated to all our factors.

Promotion was related only to two HSNS factors, but the relationship was positive not negative, whereas assessment was positively related to five of the seven NPI factors (the exceptions were Exhibitionism and Superiority) and to both HSNS factors.

Finally, locomotion was related to all factors except the HSNS Narcissistic self-focus one although the direction of these relationships varied. Consistent with what we expected for NPI Entitlement (if it is the narcissistic 'core'), locomotion was negatively related to this factor, as it was to HSNS Hypersensitivity. Locomotion was positively related to all other NPI factors.

Furthermore, the finding that the HSNS Narcissistic self-focus factor was unrelated to locomotion is consistent with Boldero and Bell's (2012b) finding that this factor is unrelated to self-esteem.

Table 4. Results of the Path Analyses predicting NPI and HSNS factors from Promotion, Prevention, Locomotion, and Assessment

Factor	Sample 1				Sample 2			
	Promotion	Prevention	Locomotion	Assessment	Promotion	Prevention	Locomotion	Assessment
Grandiose Narcissism	.06	.01	.44***	.16*	.38***	-.25***	.11	.12*
Vulnerable Narcissism	.20***	.09	-.23***	.42***	-.21***	.01	-.16*	.45***
NPI Exhibitionism	.05	-.01	.33***	.12	.36***	-.20***	.07	.05
NPI Self-sufficiency	.08	-.03	.31***	.14*	.31***	-.18***	.07	.22***
NPI Vanity	.04	-.01	.26***	.13*	.32***	-.15*	.01	.04
NPI Authority	-.02	.04	.34***	.19*	.37***	-.12*	-.24*	.04
NPI Exploitativeness	-.12	-.01	.37***	.19*	.23*	-.24***	.18*	.02
NPI Entitlement	.03	.02	-.39***	.14*	.38***	-.26***	.04	.10
NPI Superiority	.16	-.00	.30***	.20	.27***	-.18***	.19*	.07
HSNS Hypersensitivity	.17*	.08	-.23***	.38***	-.15*	.03	-.14*	.48***
HSNS Narcissistic Self-focus	.19*	.11	-.06	.23***	-.10	-.07	-.11	.22***

*p < .05; **p < .01; ***p < .001.
Note: Beta weights are shown.

For Sample 2, a different pattern of relationships were found. Consistent with predictions, promotion was positively associated with all NPI factors and was negatively related to HSNS Hypersensitivy. Furthermore, prevention was negatively related to all the NPI factors, locomotion was positively related to NPI Exploitativeness and Superiority and negatively related to HSNS Hypersensitivity, and assessment was positively related to NPI Self-sufficiency and to the two HSNS factors. However, the other relationships found were inconsistent with predictions.

These results need to be interpreted in light of the relatively large correlations between promotion and locomotion for these samples (Sample 1, $r = .51, p < .001$; Sample 2, $r = .32, p < .001$) and the use of the different NPI variants. Correlations of this size have been found in the past (Boldero, Higgins, & Hulbert, 2012). Thus, the failure to find that both promotion and locomotion are predictors of a factor likely reflects this correlation.[28] However, the failure to find relationships with prevention and assessment cannot be accounted for by such correlations. For the present samples, the self-regulatory factors were, at best, weakly correlated (Sample 1, $r = -.06, p = .388$; Sample 2, $r = .18, p = .013$). Rather, they suggest that the nature of the measurement of our NPI factors, like the results for attachment and parenting, might be an issue. On balance the results for Sample 2 are, once again, more consistent with our predictions than those for Sample 1.

One remaining issue is why assessment failed to predict any NPI factors except NPI Self-sufficiency. Assessment refers to comparing different alternative self-states being critical of the self and others. It is possible that the grandiose narcissism dimensions are unrelated to this factor because those high in, for example, the NPI facets of Vanity or Authority, are uncritical of themselves and their present states. The positive relationship of Self-sufficiency with assessment likely occurred because self-sufficiency requires relatively accurate knowledge of one's capabilities.

CONCLUSION

To conclude, we have presented information about the conceptualization of grandiose and vulnerable narcissism in clinical and social/personality psychology, focusing on their assessment and links. There is a consensus

---

[28] This covariation in factors likely accounts for the different patterns of relationships found for the HSNS factors across samples. Both samples completed identical HSNS versions.

that, despite the DSM-IV criteria focusing on grandiose narcissism, vulnerable narcissism is a distinct form or variant of the disorder.[29] We have also discussed issues that are part of the ongoing debate about the use of the NPI (Raskin & Hall, 1979), concluding like Miller and Campbell (2011), that these are not sufficient to preclude using this scale as a measure of grandiose narcissism.

A further, more serious issue is the instability of NPI's factor structure and the reliability its subscales. Like others (e.g., Ackerman et al., 2011), we have argued that the failure to establish a stable factor structure has occurred because the studies that have examined this structure have not used optimal techniques. We also considered whether this might be partly an issue of the format of the NPI items. Evidence from our recent studies (Boldero & Bell, 2012a) indicates that when optimal techniques are used, the NPI's structure is consistent with that found by Raskin and Terry (1989) regardless of the items' format. Specifically, seven factors that assess Exhibitionism, Self-sufficiency, Vanity, Authority, Exploitativeness, Entitlement, and Superiority are assessed by the NPI's 40 items. This structure is stable across the two NPI variants we used. These variants are those which present the narcissistic NPI statements and assess either the extent to which these are self-descriptive (as suggested by Corry et al., 2008, and Kubarych et al., 2004) or the number that are self-descriptive. These factors loaded on a second-order factor which can be thought of as a trait whereas the first-order factors can be thought of as lower-order dimensions or facets. However, the format of the items does have an impact on the subscales' internal consistency, with the Likert-scale variant outperforming the dichotomous one in this regard.

Additional evidence from our other recent studies (Boldero & Bell, 2012b) indicates that, consistent with Fossati et al. (2009) and Huprich et al. (2012), the HSNS (Hendin & Cheek, 1997) is also multi-dimensional. Further, its two lower-order factors, Hypersensitivity and Grandiose self-focus, load on a second-order factor. Significantly, the correlations of the HSNS lower-order factors with both the NPI lower-order and the second-order factors indicate that entitlement and having a narcissistic self-focus are core features shared by the two narcissism forms. In addition, these factors were negatively related to self-esteem, as was HSNS Hypersensitivity. This is consistent with the proposition that narcissistic self-regulation involves inner fragility (e.g., Morf & Rhodewalt, 2001).

---

[29] We do not engage with this discussion because our work does not provide any evidence that would inform it.

Using data from two additional samples, we were able to explore the proposed associations of both our grandiose and vulnerable narcissism traits and their lower-order dimensions with two sets of factors. The first set comprised recollections of cold and overvaluative parenting and avoidant and anxious attachment that are proposed to reflect the outcomes of early experiences with caregivers (Hazan & Shaver, 1987; Otway & Vignoles, 2006). The second comprised the promotion and prevention self-regulatory concerns and the locomotion and assessment goal pursuit processes that are also thought to develop in interactions with caregivers (Higgins & Silberman, 1998; Kruglanski et al., 2000).

The vulnerable narcissism trait was related to both anxious and avoidant attachment whereas grandiose narcissism was associated with overvaluative parenting, suggesting that there is no common etiology for the two narcissism forms. However, the second set of analyses suggested a common etiological factor. Both grandiose and vulnerable narcissism were positively associated with assessment. What differed between the forms were their relationships with the other self-regulatory factors. Grandiose narcissism was positively associated with promotion and negatively associated with prevention. In contrast, vulnerable narcissism was negatively associated with promotion and locomotion. Thus, consistent with Campbell and associates' (e.g., Campbell, Brunell, & Finkel, 2006; Campbell & Foster, 2007) agency model, grandiose narcissism involves a concern with the attainment of positive outcomes but lack of concern with preventing negative ones whereas vulnerable narcissism is associated with self-regulatory failure (i.e., failure to attain positive outcomes and to move from state-to-state).

Consideration of the relationships with the lower-order factors or dimensions suggested a more complex pattern of relationships that was obscured by consideration of the traits alone. For example, the self-sufficiency grandiose dimension, unlike all other dimensions, was related to avoidant attachment (Sample 2). Likewise, vulnerable narcissism as a trait was related to both anxious and avoidant attachment for both samples. However, for Sample 2, HSNS Hypersensitivity was only related to anxious attachment. Similarly, several dimensions were associated with both recollections of overvaluative and cold parenting whereas others were only associated with overvaluative parenting. Differing patterns of relationships with the self-regulatory factors were also found. For example, locomotion was negatively associated with NPI Authority and positively associated with Exploitativeness and Entitlement. Similarly, HSNS Hypersensitivity was negatively associated with both promotion and locomotion whereas

Narcissistic self-focus was not related to either self-regulatory factor. Taken together these results suggest that consideration of relationships with the dimensions of grandiose and vulnerable narcissism is a profitable line of research.

Finally, consideration of the utility of the two NPI variants is warranted. Although these both had equivalent factor structures (Boldero & Bell, 2012a & b), the Likert-scale variant appears to be more useful than the dichotomous one. Not only were the relationships uncovered using this variant more consistent with predictions, its subscales were all internally consistent. However, like the results of others who have used Raskin and Terry's (1988) forced choice variant (e.g., del Rosario & White, 2006), our dichotomous variant had subscales that were not internally consistent. This likely occurred because participants were more willing to endorse particular items as, for example, somewhat self-descriptive than endorsing an item as simply self-descriptive (as in the dichotomous variant). Thus, researchers using the NPI in the future should consider using this variant rather than either our dichotomous variant or Raskin and Terry's (1988) forced choice one.

In summary, we believe that both the NPI and the HSNS are useful measures for assessing grandiose and vulnerable narcissism, respectively. We recommend that a Likert-scale version of the NPI should be used in preference to a dichotomous one. We also recommend that researchers consider using narcissism dimensions rather than the higher-order traits as we believe that this will be a much more productive research enterprise. Their use will likely lead to new and exciting findings that will allow researchers to more fully explore the etiology and consequences of grandiose and vulnerable narcissism.

REFERENCES

Ackerman, R. A., Witt, E. A., Donnellan, M. B., Trzesniewski, K. H., Robins, R. W., & Kashy, D. A. (2011). What does the Narcisstic Personality Inventory really measure? *Assessment, 18*, 67-87.

Ainsworth, M. D. S., Blehar, M. C., Waters, E., & Wall, S. (1978). *Patterns of attachment: Assessed in the strange situation and at home.* Hillsdale, NJ: Erlbaum.

Ames, D. R., Rose, P., & Anderson, C. P. (2006). The NPI-16 as a short measure of narcissism. *Journal of Research in Personality, 40*, 440-450.

American Psychological Association. (1980). *Diagnostic and statistical manual of mental disorders* (3rd ed.). Washington, DC: Author.

American Psychological Association. (1987). *Diagnostic and statistical manual of mental disorders, revised* (3rd ed.). Washington, DC: Author.

American Psychological Association. (1994). *Diagnostic and statistical manual of mental disorders* (4th ed.). Washington, DC: Author.

Ashby, H. U. (1978). An MMPI scale for narcissistic personality disorder. *Dissertation Abstracts International, 39*, 10.

Ashby, H. U., Lee, R. R., & Duke, E. H. (1979). *A narcissistic personality disorder MMPI scale.* Paper presented at the 87th annual meeting of the American Psychological Association, New York, NY.

Atlas, G. D., & Them, M. A. (2008). Narcissism and sensitivity to criticism: A preliminary investigation. *Current Psychology, 27*, 62-76.

Barelds, D. P. H., & Dijkstra, P. (2010). Narcissistic Personality Inventory: Structure of the adapted Dutch version. *Scandinavian Journal of Psychology, 51*, 132-138.

Batholomew, K., & Horowitz, L. M. (1991). Attachment styles among young adults: A test of a four-category model. *Journal of Personality and Social Psychology, 61*, 226-244.

Besser, A., & Zeigler-Hill, V. (2010). The influence of pathological narcissism on emotional and motivational responses to negative events: The roles of visibility and concern about humiliation. *Journal of Research in Personality, 44*, 520-534.

Boldero, J. M., & Bell, R. C. (2012a). Revisiting what the Narcissistic Personality Inventory really measures: Evidence that Raskin and Terry's (1988) model does fit. *Manuscript under review*.

Boldero, J. M., & Bell, R. C. (2012b). The Hypersensitive Narcissism Scale: Factor structure and relationships with self-esteem and grandiose narcissism. *Manuscript under review*.

Boldero, J. M., & Bell, R. C. (2012c). An evaluation of the factor structure of the Problem Gambling Severity Index. *International Gambling Studies, 12*, 89-110.

Boldero, J. M., Higgins, E. T., & Hulbert, C. A. (2012). Personality, self-esteem, and self-regulatory concerns: The roles of promotion, prevention, locomotion, and assessment. *Manuscript under review*.

Bornovaloa, M. A., Fishman, S., Strong, D. R., Kruglanski, A. W., & Lejuez, C. W. (2008). Borderline personality disorder in the context of self-regulation: Understanding symptoms and hallmark features as deficits in locomotion and assessment. *Personality and Individual Differences, 44*, 22-31.

Bosson, J. K., Lakey, C. E., Campbell, W. K., Zeigler-Hill, C., Jordan, C. H., & Kernis, M. H. (2008). Untangling the links between narcissism and self-esteem: A theoretical and empirical review. *Social and Personality Compass, 2*, 1415-1439.

Bosson, J. K., & Prewitt-Freilino, J. L. (2007). Overvalued and ashamed: Considering the roles of self-esteem and self-conscious emotions in covert narcissism. In J. L. Tracy, R. W. Robins, & J. P. Tangney (Eds.), *The self-conscious emotions: Theory and research* (2nd ed., pp. 407-425). New York, NY: Guilford.

Bosson, J. K., Swann, W. B., Jr., & Pennebaker, J. (2000). Stalking the perfect measure of implicit self-esteem: The blind men and the elephant revisited? *Journal of Personality and Social Psychology, 79*, 631-643.

Bosson, J. K., & Weaver, J. R. (2011). "I love me some me": Examining the links between narcissism and self-esteem. In W. K. Campbell & J. D. Miller (Eds.), *The handbook of narcissism and narcissistic personality disorder: Theoretical approaches, empirical findings, and treatments* (pp. 261-282). Hoboken, NJ: John Wiley & Sons.

Bowlby, J. (1988). *A secure base.* New York, NY: Basic Books.

Brennan, K.A., Clark, C.L., & Shaver P.R. (1998). Self-report measurement of adult romantic attachment: An integrative overview. In J. A. Simpson & W. S. Rholes (Eds.), *Attachment theory and close relationships* (pp. 46–76), New York: Guilford.

Brown, R. P., & Bosson, J. K. (2001). Narcissus meets Sisyphus: Self-love, self-loathing, and the never-ending pursuit of self-worth. *Psychological Inquiry, 12*, 210-213.

Brown, R. P., Budzek, K., & Tamborski, M. (2009). On the meaning and measure of narcissism. *Personality and Social Psychology Bulletin, 35*, 951-964.

Brown, R. P., & Zeigler-Hill, V. (2004). Narcissism and the non-equivalence of self-esteem measures: A matter of dominance? *Journal of Research in Personality, 38*, 585-592.

Buhrmester, M. D., Blanton, H., & Swann, W. B., Jr. (2011). Implicit self-esteem: Nature, measurement, and a new way forward. *Journal of Personality and Social Psychology, 100*, 365-385.

Buss, D. M., & Chiodo, L. M. (1991). Narcissistic acts in everyday life. *Journal of Personality, 59*, 179-215.

Cain, N. M., Pincus, A. L., & Ansell, E. B. (2008). Narcissism at the crossroads: Phenotypic description of pathological narcissism across clinical theory, social/personality psychology, and psychiatric diagnosis. *Clinical Psychology Review, 28*, 638-656.

Campbell, W. K., Bonacci, A. M., Shelton, J., Exline, J. J., & Bushman, B. J. (2004). Psychological entitlement: Interpersonal consequences and validation of a self-report measure. *Journal of Personality Assessment, 83*, 29-45.

Campbell, W. K., Brunell, A. B., & Finkel, E. J. (2006). Narcissism, interpersonal self-regulation, and romantic relationships: An agency model approach. In E. J. Finkel & K. D. Vohs (Eds.), *Intrapersonal processes, interpersonal relationships* (pp. 57-83). New York: Guilford.

Campbell, W. K. & Foster, J. D. (2007). The Narcissistic self: Background, an extended agency model, and ongoing controversies. In C. Sedikides & S. Spencer (Eds.), *Frontiers in social psychology: The self* (pp. 115-138). Philadelphia: Psychology Press.

Campbell, W. K., Goodie, A. S., & Foster, J. D. (2004). Narcissism, confidence, and risk attitude. *Journal of Behavioral Decision Making, 17*, 297-311.

Campbell, W. K., Reeder, G. D., Sedikides, C., & Elliot, A. J. (2000). Among friends. An examination of friendship and self-serving bias. *British Journal of Social Psychology, 39*, 229-239.

Carroll, J.B. (1961). The nature of the data, or how to choose a correlation coefficient. *Psychometrika, 26*, 347-372.

Cattell, R. B. (1966). The scree test for the number of factors. *Multivariate Behavior Research, 1*, 245-276.

Cronbach, L. J. (1951). Coefficient alpha and the internal structure of tests. *Psychometrika, 16*, 297-334.

Church, A. T., & Burke, P. J. (1994). Exploratory and confirmatory tests of the Big Five and Tellegen's three- and four-dimensional models. *Journal of Personality and Social Psychology, 66*, 93-114.

Cohen, J. (1988). *Statistical power anlaysis for the behavioral sciences* (2nd ed.). New Jersey: Lawrence Erlbaum Associates.

Corry, N., Merritt, R. D., Mrug, S., & Pamp, B. (2008). The factor structure of the Narcissistic Personality Inventory. *Journal of Personality Assessment, 90*, 593-560.

Costello, A. B., & Osbourne, J. W. (2005). Best practices in exploratory factor analysis: Four recommendations for getting the most from your analysis. *Practical Assessment, Research & Evaluation, 10* (7). Available online: http://pareonline.net/getvn.asp? v=10& n=7

Crawford, C.B., and Koopman, P. (1973). A note on Horn's test for the number of factors in factor analysis. *Multivariate Behavioral Research, 8*, 117-125.

Crawford, C.B., and Koopman, P. (1979). Inter-rater reliability of scree test and mean square ratio test of numbers of factors. *Perceptual and Motor Skills, 49*, 223-226.

del Rosario, P. M., & White, R. M. (2005). The Narcissistic Personality Inventory: Test-retest stability and internal consistency. *Personality and Individual Differences, 39*, 1075-1081.

Dickinson, K. A., & Pincus, A. L. (2003). Interpersonal analysis of grandiose and vulnerable narcissism. *Journal of Personality Disorders, 17*, 188-207.

DiStefano, C., & Motl, R. W. (2006). Further investigating method effects associated with negatively worded items on self-report surveys. *Structural Equation Modeling, 13*, 440-464.

DiStefano, C., & Motl, R. W. (2009). Personality correlates of method effects due to negatively worde items on the Rosenberg Self-Esteem scale. *Personality and Individual Differences,46*, 309-313.

Egan, V., & Lewis, M. (2011). Narcissism and agreeableness differentiate emotional and narcissistic expressions of aggression. *Personality and Individual Differences, 50*, 845-850.

Egan, V., & McCorkindale, C. (2007). Narcissism, vanity, personality and mating effort. *Personality and Individual Differences, 43*, 2105-2115.

Emmons, R. A. (1984). Factor analysis and construct validity of the Narcissistic Personality Inventory. *Journal of Personality Assessment, 48*, 291–299.

Emmons, R. A. (1987). Narcissism: Theory and measurement. *Journal of Personality and Social Psychology, 52*, 11-17.

Fabrigar, L. R., Wegener, D. T., MacCallum, R. C., & Strahan, E. J. (1999). Evaluating the use of exploratory factor analysis in psychological research. *Psychological Methods, 4*, 272-299.

Fossati, A., Beauchaine, T. P., Grazioli, F., Carretta, I., Cortinovis, F., & Maffei, C. (2005). A latent structure analysis of Diagnostic and Statistical Manual of Mental Disorders, narcissistic personality disorder criteria. *Comprehensive Psychiatry, 46*, 361-367.

Fossati, A., Borroni, S., Eisenberg, N., & Maffei, C. (2010). Relations of proactive and reactive dimensions of aggression to overt and covert narcissism in nonclinical adolescents. *Aggressive Behavior, 36*, 21-27.

Fossati, A., Borroni, S., Grazioloi, F., Dornetti, L., Marcassoli, I., Maffei, C., & Cheek, J. (2009). Tracking the hypersensitive dimension in narcissism: Reliability and validity of the Hypersensitivie Narcissism Scale. *Personality and Mental Health, 3*, 235-247.

Foster, J. D., & Campbell, W. K. (2007). Are there such things as "Narcissistics" in social psychology? A taxometric analysis of the Narcissistic Personality Inventory. *Personality and Individual Differences, 43*, 1321-13332.

Foster, J. D., & Trimm, R. F. (2008). On being eager and uninhibited: Narcissism and approach-avoidance motivation. *Personality and Social Psychology Bulletin, 34*, 1004-1017.

Fraley, R. C., Waller, N. G., & Brennan, K. A. (2000). An item-response theory analysis of self-report measures of adult attachment. *Journal of Personality and Social Psychology, 78*, 350-365.

Freud, S. (1957). On narcissism: An introduction. In J. Strachey (Ed. and Trans.), *The standard edition of the complete works of Sigmund Freud* (Vol. 14, pp. 67-104). London: Hogarth. (Original work published 1914).

Friedman, R. S., & Förster, J. (2001). The effects of promotion and prevention cues on creativity. *Journal of Personality and Social Psychology, 81*, 1001-1013.

Grant, H., & Higgins, E. T. (2003). Optimism, promotion pride, and prevention pride as predictors of quality of life. *Personality and Social Psychology Bulletin, 29*, 1521-1532.

Greenwald, A. G., McGee, D. E., & Schwartz, J. K. L. (1998). Measuring individual differences in implicit cognition: The implicit association test. *Journal of Personality and Social Psychology, 74*, 1464-1480.

Gregg, A. P., & Sedikides, C. (2010). Narcissistic fragility: Rethinking its links to explicit and implicit self-esteem. *Self and Identity, 9*, 142-161.

Gunderson, G. G., Ronningstam, E., & Smith, L. E. (1995). Narcissistic personality disorder. In W. J. Livesley (Ed.), *The DSM-IV personality disorders* (pp. 201-212). New York, NY: Guilford Press.

Halama, P. (2008). Confirmatory factor analysis of Rosenberg Self-Esteem Scale in a sample of Slovak high school and university students. *Studia Psychologica, 50*, 255-266.

Hazan, C., & Shaver, P. (1987). Romantic love conceptualized as an attachment process. *Journal of Personality and Social Psychology, 52*, 511-524.

Helmreich, R., Stapp, J., & Ervin, C (1974). The Texas Social Behavior Inventory (TSBI): An objective measure of self-esteem or social competence. *Catalog of Selected Documents in Psychology, 4*, 79, MS. 681.

Hendin, H. M., & Cheek, J. M. (1997). Assessing hypsensitive narcissism: A reexamination of Murray's Narcism Scale. *Journal of Research in Personality, 31*, 588-599.

Higgins, E. T. (1997). Beyond pleasure and pain. *American Psychologist, 52*, 1280-1300.

Higgins, E. T. (2008). Culture and personality: Variability across universal motives as the missing link. *Social and Personality Compass, 2*, 608-634.

Higgins, E. T., & Silberman, I. (1998). Development of regulatory focus: Promotion and prevention as ways of living. In J. Heckhausen & C. S. Dweck (Eds.), *Motivation and self-regulation across the life span* (pp. 78-113). New York, NY: Cambridge University Press.

Higgins, E. T., Friedman, R. S., Harlow, R. E., Idson, L. C., Adyuk, O. N., & Taylor, A. (2001). Achievement orientations from subjective histories of success: Promotion vs. prevention pride. *European Journal of Social Psychology, 31, 3-23.*

Higgins, E. T., Kruglanski, A. W., & Pierro, A. (2003). Regulatory mode: Locomotion and assessment as distinct orientations. In M. P. Zanna (Ed.), *Advances in experimental social psychology* (Vol. 35, pp. 293-344). New York: Academic Press.

Horn, J. L. (1965). A rationale and test for the number of factors in factor analysis. *Psychometrika, 30,* 179-185.

Horton, R. S. (2011). Parenting as a cause of narcissism: Empirical support for psychodynamic and social learning theories. In W. K. Campbell & J. D. Miller (Eds.), *The handbook of narcissism and narcissistic personality disorder: Theoretical approaches, empirical findings, and treatments* (pp. 181-190). Hoboken, NJ: John Wiley & Sons.

Horton, R. S., Bleau, G., & Drweci, B. (2006). Parenting narcissus: What are the links between parenting and narcissism? *Journal of Personality, 74*, 345-376.

Huprich, S., Luchner, A., Roberts, C., & Poulit, G. (2012). Understanding the association between depressive personality and hypersensitive (vulnerable) narcissism: Some preliminary findings. *Personality and Mental Health, 6,* 50-60.

Huprich, S. K., Margrett, J. E., Barthelemy, K. J., & Fine, M. A. (1996). The Depressive Personality Inventory: An initial investigation of its psychometric properties. *Journal of Clinical Psychology, 52,* 153-159.

Hyler, S. E. (1994). *Personality Diagnostic Questionnaire-4.* New York: New York State Psychiatric Institute.

Jordan, C. H., Spencer, S. J., Zanna, M. P., Hoshino-Browne, E., & Correll, J. (2003). Secure and defensive high self-esteem. *Journal of Personality and Social Psychology, 85,* 969-978.

Kaiser, H. F. (1960). The application of electronic computers to factor analysis. *Educational and Psychological Measurement, 20,* 141-151.

Kansi, J. (2003). The Narcissistic Personality Inventory: Applicability in a Swedish population sample. *Scandinavian Journal of Psychology, 44,* 441-448.

Kernberg, O. (1975). *Borderline conditions and pathological narcissism.* New York: Aronson.

Kitayama, S., & Karasawa, M. (1997). Implicit self-esteem in Japan: Name letters and birthday numbers. *Personality and Social Psychology Bulletin, 23,* 736-742.

Kohut, H. (1971). *The analysis of the self.* Madison, WI: International Universities Press.

Kohut, H. (1977). *The restoration of the self.* Madison, WI: International Universities Press.

Krizan, Z. (2008). What is implicit about implicit self-esteem? *Journal of Research in Personality, 42,* 1635-1640.

Kruglanski, A. W., Orehek, E., Higgins, E. T., Pierro, A., & Shalev, I. (2010). Modes of self-regulation: Assessment and locomotion as independent determinants of goal pursuit. In R. H. Hoyle (Ed.), *Handbook of personality and self-regulation* (pp. 375-402). Malden, MA: Blackwell Publishing.

Kruglanski, A. W., Thompson, E. P., Higgins, E. T., Atash, M. N., Pierro, A., Shah, J. Y., & Speigel, S. (2000). To "do the right think" or "just do it": Locomotion and assessment as distinct self-regulatory imperatives. *Journal of Personality and Social Psychology, 79,* 793-815.

Kubarych, T. S., Deary, I. J., & Austin, E J. (2004). The Narcissistic Personality Inventory: Factor structure in a non-clinical sample. *Personality and Individual Differences, 36*, 857-872.

Lakey, C. E., Rose, P., Campbell, W. K., & Goodie, A. S. (2008). Probing the link between narcissism and gambling: The mediating role of judgment and decision-making bias. *Journal of Behavioral Decision Making, 21*, 113-137.

Levy, K. N., Ellison, W. D., & Reynoso, J. S. (2011). A historical review of narcissism and narcissistic personality. In W. K. Campbell & J. D. Miller (Eds.), *The handbook of narcissism and narcissistic personality disorder: Theoretical approaches, empirical findings, and treatments* (pp. 3-13). Hoboken, NJ: John Wiley & Sons.

Liberman, N., Idson, L. C., Camacho, C. J., & Higgins, E. T. (1999). Promotion and prevention choices between stability and change. *Journal of Personality & Social Psychology, 77*, 1135-1145.

Lord, F. M., & Novick, M. R. (1968). *Statistical theories of mental test scores*. Reading, MA: Addison-Wesley.

Luchner, A. F., Houston, J. M., Walker, C., & Houston, M. A. (2011). Exploring the relationship between two forms of narcissism and competitiveness. *Personality and Individual Differences, 51*, 779-782.

Lynam, D. R., & Widiger, T. A. (2001). Using the five-factor model to represent the DSM-IV personality disorders: an expert consensus approach. *Journal of Abnormal Psychology, 110*, 401-12.

Marsh, H. W., Lüdtke, O., Muthén, B. O., Asparouhov, T., Morin, A. J. S., Trautwein, U., & Nagengast, B. (2010). A new look at the Big Five Factor structure through exploratory structural equation modeling. *Psychological Assessment, 22*, 471-491.

Maxwell, K., Donnellan, M. B., Hopwood, C. J., & Ackerman, R. A. (2011). Two faces of Narcissus? An empirical comparison of the Narcissistic Personality Inventory and the Pathological Narcissism Inventory. *Personality and Individual Differences, 50*, 577-582.

Meyer, B., & Pilkonis (2005). An attachment model of personality disorders. In M. F. Lezenweger & J. F. Clarkin (Eds.), *Major theories of personality disorder* (2nd ed., pp. 231-281). New York, NY: Guilford Press.

Meyer, B., & Pilkonis, P. A. (2011). Attachment theory and narcissistic personality disorder. In W. K. Campbell & J. D. Miller (Eds.), *The handbook of narcissism and narcissistic personality disorder:*

Theoretical approaches, empirical findings, and treatments (pp. 434-444). Hoboken, NJ: John Wiley & Sons.

Miller, J. D., & Campbell, W. K. (2008). Comparing clinical and social-personality conceptualizations of narcissism. *Journal of Personality, 76,* 449-476.

Miller, J. D., & Campbell, W. K. (2010). The case for using research on trait narcissism as a building block for understanding narcissistic personality disorder. *Personality Disorders: Theory, Research, and Treatment, 1,* 180-191.

Miller, J. D., & Campbell. W. K. (2011). Addressing criticisms of the Narcissistic Personality Inventory (NPI). In W. K. Campbell & J. D. Miller (Eds.), *The handbook of narcissism and narcissistic personality disorder: Theoretical approaches, empirical findings, and treatments* (pp. 146-152). Hoboken, NJ: John Wiley & Sons.

Miller, J. D., Dir, A., Gentile, B., Wilson, L., Pryor, L. R., & Campbell, W. K. (2010). Searching for a vulnerable dark triad: Comparing factor 2 psychopathy, vulnerable narcissism, and borderline personality disorder. *Journal of Personality, 78,* 1529-1564.

Miller, J. D., Gaughan, E. T., Pryor, L. R., Kamen, C., & Campbell W. K. (2009). Is research using the Narcissistic Personality Inventory relevant for understanding narcissistic personality disorder? *Journal of Research in Personality, 43,* 483-488.

Miller, J. D., Hoffman, B. J., Campbell, W. K., & Pilkonis, P. A. (2008). An examination of the factor structure of DSM-IV narcissistic personality disorder criteria: One or two factors? *Comprehensive Psychiatry, 49,* 141-145.

Miller, J. D., Hoffman, B. J., Gaughan, E. T., Gentile, B., Maples, J., & Campbell, W. K. (2011a). Grandiose and vulnerable narcissism: A nomological network analysis. *Journal of Personality, 79,* 1013-1042.

Miller, J. D., & Maples, J. (2011). Trait models of narcissistic personality disorder, grandiose narcissism, and vulnerable narcissism. In W. K. Campbell & J. D. Miller (Eds.), *The handbook of narcissism and narcissistic personality disorder: Theoretical approaches, empirical findings, and treatments* (pp. 71-88). Hoboken, NJ: John Wiley & Sons.

Miller, J. D., Maples, J., & Campbell, W. K. (2011b). Comparing the construct validity of scales derived from the Narcissistic Personality Inventory: A reply to Rosenthal and Hooley (2010). *Journal of Research in Personality, 45,* 401-407.

Miller, J. D., Price, J., & Campbell, W. K. (2012). Is the Narcissistic Personality Inventory still relevant? A test of independent grandiosity and entitlement scales in the assessment of narcissism. *Assessment, 19,* 8-13.

Millon, T. (1981). *Disorders of personality: DSM III: Axis II.* Chichester, UK: John Wiley.

Millon, T. (1996). *Disorders of personality: DSM-IV and beyond* (2nd ed.). Oxford, England: John Wiley & Sons.

Morf, C. C., & Rhodewalt, F. (2001). Unraveling the paradoxes of narcissism: A dynamic self-regulatory processing model. *Psychological Inquiry, 12,* 177-196.

Murray, H. A. (1938). *Explorations in personality: A clinical and experimental study of fifty men of college age.* New York: Oxford University Press.

Muthén, B., & Hofacker, C. (1988). Testing the assumptions underlying tetrachoric correlations. *Psychometrika, 53,* 563-578.

Muthén, L. K., & Muthén, B. O. (1988-2011). *Mplus user's guide (6th ed.).* Los Angeles: Author.

Otway, L. J., & Vignoles, V. L. (2006). Narcissism and childhood recollections: A quantitative test of psychoanalytic predictions. *Personality and Social Psychology Bulletin, 32,* 104-116.

Paulhus, D. L., & Williams, K. M. (2002). The dark triad of personality: Narcissism, Machiavellianism, and psychopathy. *Journal of Research in Personality, 36,* 556-563.

Paulhus, D. L., Harms, P. D., Bruce, M. N., & Lysy, D. C. (2003). The over-claiming technique: Measuring bias independent of accuracy. *Journal of Personality and Social Psychology, 84,* 681-693.

Pelham, B. W., & Swann, W. B. Jr (1989). From self-conceptions to self-worth: On the sources and structure of global self-esteem. *Journal of Personality and Social Psychology, 57,* 672-680.

Pincus, A. L. (2011). Some comments on nomology, diagnostic process, and narcissistic personality disorder in the DSM-5 proposal for personality and personality disorders. *Personality Disorders: Theory, Research, and Treatment, 2,* 41-53.

Pincus, A. L., Ansell, E. M., Pimentel, C. A., Cain, N. M., Wright, A. G. C., & Levy, K. M. (2009). Initial construction and validation of the Pathological Narcissism Inventory. *Psychological Assessment, 21,* 365-379.

Pincus, A. L., & Lukowitsky, M. R. (2010). Pathological narcissism and narcissistic personality disorder. *Annual Review of Clinical Psychology, 6*, 421-446.

Rank, O. (1971). *The double: A psychoanalytic study* (H. Tucker Jr., Trans.). Chapel Hill, NC. UNC Press. (Original work published 1911).

Raskin, R. N., & Hall, C. S. (1979). A narcissistic personality inventory. *Psychological Reports, 45*, 590.

Raskin, R., & Hall, C. S. (1981). The Narcissistic Personality Inventory: Alternate form reliability and further evidence of construct validity. *Journal of Personality Assessment, 45*, 159-162.

Raskin, R., & Terry, H. (1988). A principal-components analysis of the Narcissistic Personality Inventory and further evidence of its construct validity. *Journal of Personality and Social Psychology, 54*, 890-902.

Rathvon, N., & Holmstrom, R. W. (1996). An MMPI-2 portrait of narcissism. *Journal of Personality Assessment, 66*, 1-19.

Reise, S. P., Waller, N. G., & Comrey, A. L. (2000). Factor analysis and scale revision. *Psychological Assessment, 12*, 287-297.

Reynolds, E. K., & Lejuez, C. W. (2011). Narcissism in the DSM. In W. K. Campbell & J. D. Miller (Eds.), *The handbook of narcissism and narcissistic personality disorder: Theoretical approaches, empirical findings, and treatments* (pp. 14-21). Hoboken, NJ: John Wiley & Sons.

Ronningstam, E. (2005). *Identifying and understanding narcissistic personality.* New York: Oxford University Press.

Ronningstam, E. (2009). Narcissistic personality disorder: Facing DSM-V. *Psychiatric Annals, 39*, 111-121.

Ronningstam, E. F., & Gunderson, J. G. (1990). Identifying criteria for narcissistic personality disorder. *American Journal of Psychiatry, 147*, 918– 922.

Rose, P. (2002). The happy and unhappy faces of narcissism. *Personality and Individual Differences, 33*, 379-392.

Rosenberg, M. (1965). *Society and the adolescent self-image.* Princeton, NJ: Princeton University Press.

Rosenthal, S. A., & Hooley, J. M. (2010). Narcissism assessment in social-personality research: Does the association between narcissism and psychological health result from a confound with self-esteem? *Journal of Research in Personality, 44*, 453-465.

Rosenthal, S. A., Montoya, R. M., Ridings, L. E., Rieck, S. M., & Hooley, J. M. (2011). Further evidence of the Narcissistic Personality Inventory's validity problems: A meta-analytic investigation – Response to Miller,

Maples, and Campbell (this issue). *Journal of Research in Personality, 45*, 408-416.

Russ, E., Shedler, J., Bradley, R., & Westen, D. (2008). Refining the construct of narcissistic personality disorder: Diagnostic criteria and subtypes. *American Journal of Psychiatry, 165*, 1473-1481.

Ryan, K. M., Weikel, K., & Sprechini, G. (2008). Gender differences in narcissism and courtship violence. *Sex Roles, 58*, 802-813.

Samuel, D. B., & Widiger, T. A. (2004). Clinicians' personality descriptions of prototypic personality disorders. *Journal of Personality Disorders, 18*, 286-308.

Samuel, D. B., & Widiger, T. A. (2008). Convergence of narcissism measures from the perspective of general personality functioning. *Assessment, 15*, 364.

Schoenleber, M., Sadeh, N., & Verona, E. (2011). Parallel syndromes: Two dimensions of narcissism and the facets of psychopathic personality in criminally involved individuals. *Personality Disorders: Theory, Research, and Treatment, 2*, 113-127.

Sedikides, C., Rudich, E. A., Gregg, A. P., Kumashiro, M., & Rusbult, C. (2004). Are normal narcissists psychologically healthy? Self-esteem matters. *Journal of Personality and Social Psychology, 87*, 400-416.

Serkownek, K. (1975). *Subscales for scales 5 and 0 of the MMPI.* Unpublished manuscript.

Simonson, S., & Simonson, E. (2011). Comorbidity between narcissistic personality disorders and Axis I diagnosis. In W. K. Campbell & J. D. Miller (Eds.), *The handbook of narcissism and narcissistic personality disorder: Theoretical approaches, empirical findings, and treatments* (pp. 239-247). Hoboken, NJ: John Wiley & Sons.

Smolewska, K., & Dion, K. L. (2005). Narcissism and adult attachment: A multivariate approach. *Self and Identity, 4*, 59-68.

Steger, M. F. (2007). An illustration of issues in factor extraction and identification of dimensionality in psychological assessment data. *Journal of Personality Assessment, 86*, 263-272.

Streiner, D. L. (1998). Factors affecting reliability of interpretations of scree plots. *Psychological Reports, 83,* 687-694.

Tambowski, M., & Brown, R. P. (2011). The measurement of trait narcissism in social-personality research. In W. K. Campbell & J. D. Miller (Eds.), *The handbook of narcissism and narcissistic personality disorder: Theoretical approaches, empirical findings, and treatments* (pp. 133-140). Hoboken, NJ: John Wiley & Sons.

Tritt, S. M., Ryder, A. G., Ring, A. J., & Pincus, A. L. (2010). Pathological narcissism and depressive temperament. *Journal of Affective Disorders. 122*, 280-284.

Trumpeter, N., Watson, P. J., & O'Leary, B. J. (2006). Factors within multidimensional perfectionism scales: Complexity of relationships with self-esteem, narcissism, self-control, and self-criticism. *Personality and Individual Differences, 41*, 849-860.

Twenge, J. M., Konrath, S., Foster, J. D., Campbell, W. K., & Bushman, B. (2008). Egos inflating over time: A cross-temporal meta-analysis of the Narcissistic Personality Inventory. *Journal of Personality, 76*, 875-901.

Widiger, T. A. (2010). In defense of narcissistic personality traits. *Personality Disorders: Theory, Research, and Treatment, 1,* 192-194.

Wink, P. (1991). Two faces of narcissism. *Journal of Personality and Social Psychology, 61*, 590-597.

Wright, A. G. C., Lukowitsky, M. R., Pincus, A. L., & Conroy, D. E. (2010). The higher order factor structure and gender invariance of the Pathological Narcissism Inventory, *Assessment, 17*, 467-483.

Zeigler-Hill, V. (2006). Discrepancies between implicit and explicit self-esteem: Implications for narcissism and self-esteem instability. *Journal of Personality, 74*, 119-143.

Zeigler-Hill, V., & Besser, A. (2011). Humor style mediates the association between pathological narcissism and self-esteem. *Personality and Individual Differences, 50,* 1196-1201.

Zhou, R., & Pham, M. (2004). Promotion and prevention across mental accounts: When financial products dictate consumers' investment goals. *Journal of Consumer Research, 31*, 125-135.

In: New Developments in Personality ...   ISBN: 978-1-62417-118-5
Editors: A. Morel and M. Durand   © 2013 Nova Science Publishers, Inc.

Chapter 2

WHICH 5?: EXAMINING PERSONALITY PATHOLOGY WITH THE FIVE FACTOR MODEL AND PERSONALITY PSYCHOPATHOLOGY-5

Hilary L. DeShong[1]*, Stephanie N. Mullins-Sweatt[1]
and Thomas A. Widiger[2]
[1]Oklahoma State University, Department of Psychology,
Oklahoma, US
[2]University of Kentucky, Department of Psychology,
Kentucky, US

ABSTRACT

Research suggests that dimensional models are useful in the classification of maladaptive personality traits and that these models are more useful than categorical models. As a result, the personality disorder section of the DSM-5 has proposed a shift from a categorical model to a hybrid dimensional-categorical model of diagnosing personality pathology. The current study will examine the relation between the Personality Psychopathology Five (PSY-5) model of

* Correspondence may be sent to Hilary L. DeShong, Oklahoma State University, Department of Psychology, 116 North Murray Hall, Stillwater OK 74078. Phone: 405-744-2341. Fax: 405-744-8067. E-mail address: hilary.deshong@okstate.edu.

clinically-relevant personality traits taken from the MMPI-2 with the five-factor model (FFM). Participants (n = 22) were recruited from a Psychological Services Center at a Midwestern university. Clinicians working at the center were recruited if they had a client who had previously completed the NEO PI-R and the MMPI-2. The clinicians were asked to complete the Shedler and Western Assessment Procedure (SWAP-200) to assess their respective client's personality pathology. The current study indicated that both models contribute to our understanding of personality pathology, though conclusions were limited due to the size of the sample.

Keywords: Dimensional, trait, personality, personality pathology, five-factor model, PSY-5, DSM-IV-TR, DSM-5

INTRODUCTION

The American Psychiatric Association's (APA) Diagnostic and Statistical Manual of Mental Disorders-Text Revision (DSM-IV-TR; APA, 2000) currently "represents the categorical perspective that personality disorders are qualitatively distinct clinical syndromes" (APA, 2000, p. 689). The limitations of the DSM-IV-TR personality disorder (PD) diagnostic categories have been well documented, however, including an inadequate scientific base, excessive diagnostic co-occurrence, arbitrary and inconsistent diagnostic boundaries, and inadequate coverage (Clark, 2007; First et al., 2002; Livesley, 2003; Trull & Durrett, 2005; Widiger & Mullins-Sweatt, 2005; Widiger & Trull, 2007). Significant revisions are needed to address these concerns.

Bernstein, Iscan, and Maser (2007) surveyed the memberships of the *Association for Research on Personality Disorders* (ARPD) and the *International Society for the Study of Personality Disorders* (ISSPD) with respect to problems and proposals for a future diagnostic manual. Bernstein et al. (2007) concluded "a clear majority of the PD experts were dissatisfied with the current diagnostic system" (p. 536). Eighty percent of respondents indicated that "personality disorders are better understood as variants of normal personality than as categorical disease entities" (Bernstein et al., 2007, p. 542). The classification of personality disorders in DSM-5 does appear to be shifting strongly toward a hybrid dimensional-categorical model (Krueger et al., 2011). How personality disorders will appear in DSM-5 is not entirely clear, however, as the original proposal has been revised substantially. What seems clear, though, is that dimensional traits will be included as part of the diagnosis. A number of potential dimensional models exist. For example, Widiger and Simonsen (2005) identified eighteen alternative ways in which the *DSM-IV-TR* PDs could be conceptualized dimensionally.

The dimensional traits of PD currently proposed to be included in DSM-5's hybrid model include five domains of personality: negative affectivity (e.g., emotional lability), detachment (e.g., anhedonia), antagonism (e.g., deceitfulness), constraint vs. disinhibition (e.g., irresponsibility), and psychoticism (e.g., unusual beliefs) (Krueger et al., 2011). In a document released on June 21, 2011, the Personality and Personality Disorders Work Group suggested that the model "at the domain-level, bears a strong resemblance to Dr. Allan Harkness's Personality Psychopathology Five (PSY-5) model of clinically relevant personality variants" (APA, 2011, p. 1). However, a more recent release by the Work Group indicates the "proposed model represents an extension of the Five Factor Model (FFM; Costa & Widiger, 2002) of personality that specifically delineates and encompasses the more extreme and maladaptive personality variants necessary to capture dispositional feature of PDs" (APA, 2012, p. 7). The purpose of the current study is to examine the two models, specifically in relation to personality pathology.

The Personality Psychopathy Five (PSY-5)

The development of the PSY-5 constructs first began with the identification of 39 lower-order personality traits, which were considered (by the model's authors) to be the most narrow personality traits that can be identified in relation to personality disorders (Harkness, 1992). In the original set of studies, Harkness (1992) translated the diagnostic criteria of the personality disorders into lay language and had undergraduates and community volunteers organize them into groups. They were instructed to organize them together if they were very similar in the way an individual may act. Using the resulting 39 narrow traits, Harkness and McNulty (1994) developed the five broad traits that make up the Personality Psychopathy Five (PSY-5) personality model. These five traits are: aggressiveness, psychoticism, constraint, negative emotionality/neuroticism, and positive emotionality/extraversion.

Each of these domains is thought to describe a specific area of differences in individuals. Aggressiveness is the propensity of an individual to engage in aggressive behaviors and experience anger more frequently and intensely. The domain of psychoticism measures disconnection with reality. For example, an individual who experiences severe delusions would have a high psychoticism score (i.e., they are very disconnected from the world around them).

Constraint examines one's level of impulsivity. The higher an individual is in this construct, the less "impulsive" they are. Since the model was designed to measure the more maladaptive variants of personality, the name was later changed to disconstraint. Negative emotionality, or neuroticism, is an individual's propensity to experience negative emotions very strongly and to act on these feelings. Positive emotionality, or extraversion, is the propensity for an individual to experience positive emotions strongly and thus engage in behaviors that increase these feelings. Because the low end of the spectrum is thought to be more maladaptive, the name was later changed to introversion. These two changes in domain names (disconstraint and introversion) will be used through out the remainder of the chapter as the most up to date names used for this model.

In order to assess for the PSY-5 traits, Harkness, McNulty, and Ben-Porath (1995) used items from the MMPI-2 (Butcher, Dahlstrom, Graham, Tellegen, & Kaemmer, 1989) to develop scales measuring each of the five constructs. A group of trained undergraduate students sorted each item of the MMPI into one of the five PSY-5 traits or into a pile labeled "do not apply" (Harkness et al., 1995, pp. 106).

From this, only items that had at least 51% agreement were used for the preliminary set of items for the PSY- scales. Overall, 232 items passed this selection rule. If the item was in more than one PSY-5 group, it was placed in the domain scale that it fit best with so there would be no item overlap across the domain scales. Harkness and McNulty (1994) screened the pool of items and discarded a number of items for a variety of reasons (e.g., ambiguous keying, tapped more than one construct, did not correctly assess either pole of a domain, or not correctly assessing the constructs).

Twenty items were deleted due to weak or reversed item-total correlations or cross-scale correlations while another fifteen were deleted because of poor psychometric properties. Thus the final PSY-5 scale has a total of 139 questions.

Following this, a number of clinical samples and comparison nonclinical samples were used to assess the psychometric properties of each item and scale.

Overall, the scales were internally consistent and had strong convergent and discriminant validity across the different samples. Additionally, the PSY-5 scales were compared to the Multidimensional Personality Questionnaire (MPQ; Tellegen, 1982, Tellegen & Waller, 2008), which was completed by a subsample of the college population. The results indicated that the MPQ scores that should theoretically correlate highly with the PSY-5 scales did so. Overall, these results provided evidence for the construct validity and reliability of the PSY-5 scales.

Five Factor Model

The FFM was originally derived to identify those traits that are most significant in describing oneself and other persons (Digman, 1990; John & Srivastava, 1999).

Studies have generally supported the identification of five broad domains of personality: extraversion (surgency or positive affectivity) versus introversion, agreeableness versus antagonism, conscientiousness versus undependability, neuroticism (emotional instability or negative affectivity) versus emotional stability, and openness (intellect or unconventionality) versus closedness to experience (Ashton & Lee, 2001).

Each of these five broad domains has been differentiated into six more specific facets by Costa and McCrae (1995). For example, Costa and McCrae suggest that the domain of extraversion (vs. introversion) can be differentiated into the more specific facets of warmth, gregariousness, assertiveness, activity, excitement-seeking, and positive emotionality. The FFM is not without its critics (Block, 1995; Westen, 1995). However, there is a great deal of empirical support for the construct validity of the facet and domain levels of the FFM.

This has been shown with convergent and discriminant validation in self-report, peer ratings, and spouse ratings (McCrae, Stone, Fagan, & Costa, 1998); temporal stability (McCrae & Costa, 2003); generalizability across age, gender, and culture (Digman, 1990; McCrae & Allik, 2002); and heritability (Jang, McCrae, Angleitner, Rieman, & Livesley, 1998; Loehlin, McCrae, Costa, & John, 1998).

The FFM also has been used successfully as an integrative model for personality description in a number of applied fields, including health psychology (Artistico, Baldassarri, Lauriola, & Laicardi, 2000) and industrial organizational psychology (Hogan & Holland, 2003) as well as developmental research such as child and adolescent studies (Shiner, 1998) and aging (Costa, McCrae, & Siegler, 1999).

Comparison of PSY-5 and FFM

While the FFM was developed as a model of general personality, the PSY-5 was developed specifically as a dimensional factor of personality pathology. Unlike the FFM, the PSY-5 domains do not assess lower-order facets (Quilty & Bagby, 2007). However, the domain levels of the PSY-5 and the FFM do share some similarities. Harkness et al. (1995) argued "Because the PSY-5 was developed from quantitative analyses of both normal and pathological personality (DSM-III-R Axis II) markers, the PSY-5 has both similarities to and differences from normal sample-based five-factor models" (p. 105). The PSY-5 domains of introversion and negative emotionality are in line with the FFM domains of extraversion and neuroticism, while aggressiveness and disconstraint overlap with the FFM traits of low agreeableness and low conscientiousness. Harkness et al. (1995) states that "Although PSY-5 Aggressiveness may seem to be a reflection (psychometric inversion) of normal five-factor Agreeableness, the PSY-5 markers (e.g., cruel, violent) are more extreme than normal sample-based markers of low Agreeableness (e.g., cold, unsympathetic, harsh)" (p. 105). Additionally, Harkness et al. (1995) agrees that low Disconstraint is similar to high Conscientiousness, but argues that high Disconstraint "takes on an Antisocial or Cleckley Psychopathic cast" (p. 106). Lastly, Harkness et al. (1995) argues that the PSY-5 domain of Psychoticism has no FFM counterpart.

Harkness et al. (1995) argued that the PSY-5 should be better at assessing personality pathology than the FFM because the PSY-5 constructs were developed using the diagnostic criteria for the personality disorders, which are the more maladaptive traits of personality (though it should be noted that an experimentally altered version of the NEO PI-R does adequately assess maladaptive personality functioning; Haigler & Widiger, 2001). Trull, Useda, Costa, and McCrae (1995) were the first to examine these relationships. The first study assessed the relationship of the PSY-5 domains with the FFM domains and facets in a nonclinical population. Overall, the introversion and negative emotionality scales significantly correlated with the FFM extraversion and neuroticism domains, and with each of their six facets, respectively. Additionally, the introversion scale correlated positively with the neuroticism domain and with four of the six facets (anxiety, depression, self-conscientiousness, and vulnerability). Negative emotionality was also negatively correlated with conscientiousness and all six facets of the domain, though this relationship was weaker than its relationship with neuroticism.

Aggressiveness was negatively correlated with agreeableness. It was found to correlate negatively with three specific facets (straightforwardness, compliance, and modesty). It also correlated positively with extraversion, as well as with four of its facets (gregariousness, assertiveness, activity, and excitement seeking). Disconstraint appeared to be made up of a number of facets from each domain except for neuroticism, which was not significant, though the facet impulsiveness was significant. Disconstraint negatively related to two facets of conscientiousness: dutifulness and deliberation. Additionally, disconstraint was related positively to four facets of openness (fantasy, feelings, actions, and values), negatively related to four facets of agreeableness (trust, straightforwardness, compliance, and modesty), and positively related to two facets of extraversion (excitement-seeking and positive emotions).

Lastly, psychoticism was found to significantly correlate with two facets of openness to experience (fantasy and feelings), three facets of agreeableness (trust, straightforwardness, and altruism), and one facet of conscientiousness (self-discipline). Additionally, it related to the neuroticism domain and all six facets. Trull et al. (1995) replicated these results with a clinical sample. Overall the results at the domain level showed similar results. Introversion was significantly related to both extraversion and neuroticism while negative emotionality was related to neuroticism. Additionally the relationships of aggressiveness with agreeableness, disconstraint with agreeableness and conscientiousness, and psychoticism with neuroticism were all replicated.

Lastly, the study examined the relationship of each measure with personality disorders, using a structured interview and a self-report inventory. The results showed an expected pattern. All five domains of the FFM were found to correlate with specific personality disorders, which have been found in prior studies (Costa & Widiger, 1994). The PSY-5 scales were also found to relate to specific personality disorders. In order to compare these two personality models, a series of regression analyses were performed. First, the two models were compared with the personality disorders as measured by the structured interview. Both models predicted a significant amount of variance across the disorders. Important to note, however, is that following this, the regression analyses were repeated after the BDI and BAI scores were taken into account (thus removing the impact of acute mood states on the results). After this, it was found that the PSY-5 correlated significantly with eight personality disorders while the NEO-PI scales related to seven. Again, both scales showed the ability to predict a significant amount of variance in each personality disorder, with the exception of Antisocial PD, where the PSY-5 scales accounted for twice as much variance as the FFM NEO PI scales.

For the self-report inventory, the regression analyses indicated again, both the PSY-5 and the NEO-PI were able to account for a significant amount of the variance for the PD measures. The general finding for this study was that personality disorder symptoms were related to general personality traits, fairly equally across the two models.

The studies by Trull et al. (1995) were the first to compare and contrast the PSY-5 and the FFM. A study by Bagby, Sellbom, Costa, and Widiger (2008) took this comparison a step further, by examining the incremental ability of each model across the ten personality disorders in a clinic sample. Individuals referred to a university-affiliated psychiatric facility completed the MMPI-2 (Butcher et al., 2001), NEO-PI-R (Costa & McCrae, 1992), and the Structured Clinical Interview for DSM-IV PDs Personality Questionnaire (SCID-II-PQ; First, Gibbon, Spitzer, Williams, & Benjamin, 1997). Similar results were found for the correlations between the PSY-5 and the FFM. Negative emotionality was correlated highest with neuroticism, introversion was correlated negatively with extraversion, psychoticism was correlated negatively with agreeableness, aggressiveness negatively correlated with agreeableness, and disconstraint negatively correlated with agreeableness.

Additionally, the PSY-5 and FFM domains were entered into a set of regression analyses. The first analysis used the PSY-5 and the FFM as the predictors for the 10 personality disorders. Overall, the PSY-5 accounted for more variance compared to the NEO-PI-R for paranoid, schizotypal, narcissistic, and antisocial PD, while the NEO-PI-R accounted for more of the variance for borderline, avoidant, and dependent PD. The second step of the regression tested the incremental validity of each. The NEO PI-R was found to add incremental information for paranoid, schizotypal, histrionic, narcissistic, borderline, avoidant, and dependent PD, while the PSY-5 contributed incremental information for paranoid, schizotypal, histrionic, narcissistic, borderline, and antisocial PD. Neither model was able to add significantly more information for schizoid or obsessive-compulsive PD.

Overall, this study indicates that each model may be able to predict outcomes on self-report personality disorder measures, but that each model may have strengths for certain PDs.

As can be seen from the previous literature, the FFM has been shown as a reliable and valid measure for general and pathological personality. Further comparison to the PSY-5 scales, however, is needed to further our understanding of both models and their relationships with personality pathology. The following study will assess the FFM and the PSY-5 in relation to a Q-sort personality disorder measure, the Shedler and Westen Assessment Procedure (SWAP-200; Shedler & Westen, 2004). More specifically, the following study will compare the specific facet level traits of the FFM that have been found to relate to each personality disorder to the PSY-5. This is particularly timely, given the inclusion of similar traits proposed for DSM-5.

METHODS

Participants

Participants were graduate student clinicians (n = 22; 18 female) recruited from a psychological services center at a major Midwestern university who had recently treated or were currently treating adult clients. The clinicians had a mean age of 28.82 (SD = 4.67), with a range of 23 to 39. Clinicians had an average of 4.24 (SD = 1.30) years in the doctoral program, ranging from 2 to 6 years. All clinicians were Caucasian. The clinicians' marital statuses included single (45.5%), married (50.0%) and divorced (4.5%). In terms of therapy orientation, most clinicians provided more than one specific type, with the majority including cognitive behavioral (68.2%) as their primary mode of therapy. Neurobiological (27.3%) and interpersonal (22.7%) orientations were also frequently endorsed. Additional orientations listed included cognitive (13.6%), humanistic (13.6%), psychodynamic (9.1%), and other (18%).

The clinicians obtained archival information from the records of their respective (current or previous) clients and provided the de-identified information to the researchers. The participants described 22 clients (13 women) with a mean age of 30.15 (SD = 11.12), ranging from 18-53. The majority of clients were Caucasian (86.4%), followed by Asian (9.1%) and Hispanic (4.5%). The clients had an average of 23.81 sessions (SD = 26.74), ranging between 5 and 112 sessions. The majority of clients were single (59.1%), while the rest identified as married (9.1%), divorced (13.6%) or other (9.1%). There was a wide variety in clinical diagnoses. Overall, Major Depressive Disorder was the most common primary diagnosis given alone (9.1%) and with other comorbid disorders (40.9%). There were a number of clients who were diagnosed with an anxiety disorder (45.5%), including Generalized Anxiety Disorder, Obsessive Compulsive Disorder, Post Traumatic Stress Disorder, Social Phobia, and Anxiety Disorder, Not Otherwise Specified. Additionally, a number of other primary diagnoses provided were personality disorders, including borderline, narcissistic, histrionic, paranoid, and avoidant. Lastly, other diagnoses included adjustment disorder, substance abuse, conversion disorder, and anorexia nervosa.

The clinicians also provided psychotropic medications that the clients were taking. Overall, 9 of the 22 clients (40.9%) were not taking any medications at the time of the study while the other 13 clients were taking one or more types of medications. The majority of clients were taking an SSRI (54.5%) and/or an anti-anxiety medication (22.7%). In addition, a variety of other medications were also reported, including atypical antidepressants (9.1%), antipsychotics (9.1%), stimulants (9.1%), mood stabilizer (4.5%), and/or a sleeping aid medication (4.5%).

MEASURES

Demographic Form

Each clinician completed a demographic information sheet that included their gender, age, year in program, ethnicity, martial status, and theoretical orientation.

Client History Form

Therapists also completed a clinical history form describing their respective clients, which included the gender, age, ethnicity, martial status, number of sessions, diagnosis, and psychotropic medications being taken by the client.

Minnesota Multiphasic Inventory 2 (MMPI-2; Butcher et al., 2001)

The MMPI-2 is a 567 self-report questionnaire designed to assess personality traits and psychopathology and includes the PSY-5 scales developed by Harkness et al (1995). Each PSY-5 scale assesses one of five domains of the PSY-5: aggressiveness (18 items), psychoticism (25 items), disconstraint (29 items), negative emotionality/neuroticism (33 items), and introversion/low positive emotionality (34 items). The scales were constructed using a panel of trained raters. These raters nominated items from the MMPI-2 to reflect each dimension of the PSY-5. The PSY-5 scales have been found to have internal consistency values ranging from .68 to .84 along with good convergent validity with other scales measuring similar traits and constructs (Harkness et al., 1995; McNulty, Harkness, & Ben-Porath, 1998) and with therapist-rated symptom indexes (Rouse, 1997). There have been studies indicating the usefulness of the PSY-5 scales for personality disorders (McNulty, Ben-Porath, & Watt, 1997), substance abuse (Rouse, Butcher, & Miller, 1997), and for understanding both inpatient and outpatient psychopathology (Eggers, Derksen, & DeMey, 1997).

NEO-Personality Inventory-Revised (NEO PI-R; Costa & McCrae, 1992)

The NEO-PI-R is a 240-item standardized, self-report measure designed to assess an individual's general personality functioning. Participants rate each item on a 5-point Likert scale, ranging from 1 (disagree strongly) to 5 (agree strongly). It is comprised of five domains (neuroticism, extraversion, openness to experience, agreeableness, and conscientiousness), as well as six narrower facets within each domain (e.g., trust, straightforwardness, altruism, compliance, modesty, and tender-mindedness are facets of agreeableness). Internal consistency coefficients for the domain scales have ranged from .86 (agreeableness) to .92 (neuroticism).

Shedler and Westen Assessment Procedure (SWAP-200; Shedler & Westen, 2004)

The SWAP is a 200-item Q-sort task designed to assess the extent to which clients have maladaptive personality features. To describe an individual using the SWAP-200, a rater arranges the items into eight categories, from those that are not descriptive of the individual (assigned a value of 0) to those that are highly descriptive (assigned a value of 7), using a fixed distribution, where half (100) of the items must be provided a ranking of 0, 22 items must be provided a ranking of 1, 18 items must be provided a ranking of 2, 16 items must be provided a ranking of 3, 14 items must be provided a ranking of 4, 12 items must be provided a ranking of 5, 10 items must be provided a ranking of 6, and 8 items must be provided a ranking of 7. The SWAP-200 includes assessment scales for each of the ten personality disorder diagnostic categories of the DSM-IV-TR (APA, 2000). The SWAP-200 has been shown to have good inter-rater reliability, ranging from .76 to .96 (Marin-Avellan, McGauley, Campbell, & Fonagy, 2005; Westen & Muderrisoglu, 2003, 2006). In addition, the SWAP-200 has been found to relate highly to the five factor model (Mullins-Sweatt & Widiger, 2007).

PROCEDURE

Once written informed consent from the clinician was obtained, he/she was asked to describe an adult client who has previously completed the NEO PI-R and the MMPI-2 (for clients who had provided permission for use of their archival data for research purposes as part of the clinic's initial intake procedure). The clinician then completed the one-page demographic sheet and client history form.

Following this, the clinician completed the SWAP-200 in regards to describing their respective client. Lastly, the clinicians provided the de-identified NEO PI-R and MMPI-2 previously completed by the client. All clinicians were paid 25 dollars for competing the study.

RESULTS

Table 1 provides the descriptive statistics and reliability coefficients of the NEO PI-R domains, PSY-5 domain scales and the SWAP-200 personality disorder scales. The alpha values of the NEO-PI-R domain scales ranged from .72 (openness and agreeableness) to .86 (neuroticism), while the PSY-5 scales had alpha values ranging from .62 (psychoticism) to .86 (positive emotionality). The SWAP-200 had alpha values that ranged from .42 (narcissism) to .88 (compulsive). Table 2 provides the domain correlations of the NEO PI-R with the PSY-5.

As expected, neuroticism, extraversion, and agreeableness related significantly with negative emotionality, positive emotionality, and aggressiveness, respectively. However, openness to experience was not related significantly to psychoticism and conscientiousness was not related to constraint. Discriminant correlations were also problematic. As can be seen in Table 3, each personality disorder was significantly related to domains of the PSY-5 and the NEO PI-R. However, there were a number of domain scales found to not have significant correlations with any PD. Specifically, the negative emotionality scale of the PSY-5 and the openness scale of the NEO-PI-R were not significantly related to any of the personality disorders as measured by the SWAP-200. Each personality disorder was significantly related to specific domains, and these relationships were similar to previous findings in the literature (Bagby et al., 2008; Mullins-Sweatt & Widiger, 2007) though, there were fewer significant relationships found, likely due to the small sample size. Expected relationships included schizoid PD with

Table 1. Mean and standard deviation values of the NEO-PI-R, PSY-5, and SWAP-200

	Mean	Standard Deviation	Coefficient Alpha
NEO PI-R			
Neuroticism	19.57	6.31	.86
Extraversion	17.25	6.45	.82
Openness	21.48	5.92	.71
Agreeableness	20.03	5.38	.72
Conscientiousness	17.84	5.54	.85
PSY-5			
Positive Emotionality	0.40	0.45	.86
Negative Emotionality	0.30	0.41	.80
Aggressiveness	0.63	0.44	.70
Psychoticism	0.52	0.46	.62
Disconstraint	0.57	0.46	.64
SWAP-200			
Paranoid	1.91	2.01	.75
Schizoid	1.99	2.14	.72
Histrionic	1.78	1.94	.69
Narcissistic	1.32	1.84	.42
Borderline	2.47	2.19	.56
Antisocial	1.25	1.71	.79
Avoidant	3.00	2.32	.80
Dependent	2.01	2.14	.76
Obsessive-Compulsive	2.47	2.11	.88

Table 2. Correlations of NEO-PI-R scales with PSY-5 scales

	Neg Em	Pos Em	Psy	Agg	Con
Neuroticism	.57*	-.72**	.05	-.35	.10
Extraversion	-.59*	.66**	-.44	-.04	-.19
Openness	-.21	.22	.19	-.17	-.47*
Agreeableness	-.36	-.58*	-.60**	-.46*	-.29
Conscientiousness	.07	.27	-.21	.41	.18

Note. * = p < .05; ** = p < .01; Neg Em = Negative Emotionality; Pos Em = Positive
  Emotionality; Psy = Psychoticism; Agg = Aggressiveness; Con = Constraint;
  Neur = Neuroticism; Extra = Extraversion; Open = Openness; Agree =
  Agreeableness; Consc = Conscientiousness.

PSY-5 introversion and FFM (low) extraversion, histrionic with FFM
extraversion, borderline with FFM neuroticism, antisocial with PSY-5
aggressiveness and FFM (low) agreeableness, and obsessive compulsive with
FFM conscientiousness. However, this was not the case for all PDs.

For example, while avoidant PD also was significantly related with FFM
(low) extraversion, the expected relationship with FFM neuroticism was not
found.

To determine the unique predictive values for each model in predicting
the SWAP-200 personality disorder scales, we conducted two hierarchical
regression analyses.

The PSY-5 domain scales were compared to the respective facets of the
NEO PI-R that are predicted to relate with each of the personality disorders
(Bagby et al., 2008; Trull et al., 1995). The first regression analysis employed
the PSY-5 scales in step one and then the PSY-5 and the respective NEO-PI-
R facets in step two.

As can be seen in Table 4, the NEO PI-R facets accounted for more of
the variance above and beyond the PSY-5 specifically for seven of the nine
PDs reported in this study ranging from 19% (PAR) to 74% (HST).
However, the majority of these analyses were not significant.

The second hierarchical regression employed the NEO PI-R facets in
step one and then the NEO-PI-R and PSY-5 in step two. In this instance, the
PSY-5 accounted for an additional 1% (DEP) to 20% (BDL) of variance
above and beyond what was accounted for by the NEO-PI-R. Again,
however, most of these were not significant.

Table 3. Correlations of SWAP-200 PD scales with the NEO-PI-R scales and PSY-5 scales

	PAR	SZD	HST	NAR	BDL	ATS	AVD	DEP	CMP
Neg Em	.29	.43	-.40	.25	-.11	.06	.21	-.39	-.22
Pos Em	-.06	-.68**	.23	-.09	-.40	.06	-.73**	.13	.43
Psy	.45**	.31	-.19	.18	-.17	.30	-.21	-.33	-.19
Agg	.49*	-.18	-.31	.43	-.25	.62**	-.46**	-.28	-.06
Con	.41	.23	-.05	.61**	.14	.21	.11	-.28	-.27
NEO									
Neur	-.15	.05	.32	-.17	.39*	-.17	.21	.12	-.08
Extra	-.03	-.54**	.38*	.03	-.19	.09	-.44*	.37*	.12
Open	-.05	-.25	.17	-.26	-.21	.11	-.15	.27	-.13
Agree	-.33	-.27	.11	-.14	-.07	-.42*	.05	.22	.13
Consc	.13	-.12	.41*	.05	-.33	-.11	-.13	-.25	.37*

Note. * = p < .05; ** = p < .01; PAR = Paranoid PD; SZD = Schizoid PD; HST = Histrionic PD; NAR = Narcissistic PD; BDL = Borderline PD; ATS = Antisocial PD; AVD = Avoidant PD; DEP = Dependent PD; CMP = Obsessive-Compulsive PD; Neg Em = Negative Emotionality; Pos Em = Positive Emotionality; Psy = Psychoticism; Agg = Aggressiveness; Con = Constraint; Neur = Neuroticism; Extra = Extraversion; Open = Openness; Agree = Agreeableness; Consc = Conscientiousness.

Table 4. Regression analyses of the PSY-5 domains and the NEO-PI-R facets in predicting SWAP PD scales

	PAR ΔR^2	SZD ΔR^2	HST ΔR^2	NAR ΔR^2	BDL ΔR^2	ATS ΔR^2	AVD ΔR^2	DEP ΔR^2	CMP ΔR^2
Step 1: PSY-5 Step 2: PSY-5 and NEO-PI-R									
1. PSY-5	.10	.47*	.13	.19	.02	.41*	.63**	.15	.07
2. PSY-5; NEO	.19	.22	.74	.42	.67	.57**	.16	.66	.47
Total R²	.29	.69	.86	.61	.69	.98	.79	.81	.54
Step 1: NEO-PI-R; Step 2: NEO-PI-R and PSY-5									
1. NEO	.21	.55*	.79	.72*	.49	.78	.70	.80	.50
2. NEO; PSY-5	.08	.14	.08	.04	.20	.19**	.09	.01	.03
Total R²	.29	.69	.86	.76	.69	.99	.79	.81	.53

Note. * = p < .05; ** = p < .01; PSY-5 = Personality Psychopathy Five; NEO = NEO-Personality Inventory-Revised; PAR = Paranoid PD; SZD = Schizoid PD; HST = Histrionic PD; NAR = Narcissistic PD; BDL = Borderline PD; ATS = Antisocial PD; AVD = Avoidant PD; DEP = Dependent PD; CMP = Obsessive-Compulsive PD.

DISCUSSION

Problems with the current diagnostic system for personality disorder are well documented throughout the literature (Clark, 2007; First et al., 2002; Livesley, 2003; Trull & Durrett, 2005; Widiger & Mullins-Sweatt, 2005; Widiger & Trull, 2007). Due to these problems, the DSM-5 Work Group is proposing significant revisions to the classification system. The new proposed model is shifting from a strictly categorical model to a hybrid categorical-dimensional model (Kruger et al., 2011) in which personality disorders are viewed as extreme maladaptive variants of general personality. There are a number of dimensional trait models that could be used to conceptualize the personality disorders. The traits that were proposed include five domains of personality: negative affectivity, detachment, antagonism, constraint vs. disinhibition, and psychoticism or peculiarity. It has been noted by the Work Group that these domains resemble the Personality Psychopathy Five (PSY-5; Harkness, Finn, McNulty, & Shields, 2011) and/or are an extension of the Five Factor Model (Costa & Widiger, 2002) of general personality (Wright et al., 2012). Specifically, DSM-5 negative affectivity appears akin to PSY-5 negative emotionality and FFM neuroticism, DSM-5 detachment to PSY-5 low positive emotionality and FFM low extraversion, DSM-5 psychoticism to PSY-5 psychoticism and FFM openness to experience, DSM-5 antagonism to PSY-5 aggressiveness and FFM low agreeableness, and DSM-5 disinhibition to PSY-5 low constraint and FFM low agreeableness. A recent study (Thomas et al., in press) examining the trait scale of the *Personality Inventory for the DSM-5* (PID-5; Krueger et al., 2011) suggest five higher order factors that correspond with the FFM.

The purpose of the current study was to examine the PSY-5 and the FFM in relation to personality pathology. The results of the current study indicate that both dimensional models are able to account for variance in personality disorders as measured by the SWAP-200. However, due to the small sample size and the use of cross-method assessment (self-report and clinician report), many of these relationships were not significant.

LIMITATIONS AND FUTURE DIRECTIONS

The primary limitation of this study was the small sample size, which greatly limited conclusions from the results. Additionally, there were some relationships that are typically found in the literature that did not reach significance in this study. For instance, paranoid PD and low agreeableness are often found to strongly correlate (Saulsman & Page, 2005), but in this study, the correlation of -.33 (often found to be a medium effect) was not significant (p = .055). There were other similar relationships that approached significance due to the small sample size. Future studies could expand upon the findings in this study by having a larger sample size with a more diverse sample.

The current study used a clinical sample with a variety of psychopathology. While this approach leads to PD prevalence rates that are externally valid, it does not ensure adequate sampling of individuals who have been assessed and diagnosed with a personality disorder. Though some of the clients did have a personality disorder diagnosis, a full range and level of severity was not represented and other clients had only Axis I diagnoses. Further research with other clinical settings (e.g., substance abuse treatment facilities, private practice, hospital) would be warranted.

These results are drawn from a single group of graduate student clinicians with very similar educational background and level of experience. Future research should be conducted within samples that vary in educational background, experience, theoretical orientation, and other demographic variables.

CONCLUSION

Given the discussion of the proposed revision to include dimensional personality traits in the upcoming diagnostic manual, it is important that studies investigate models suggested to be the basis of the new system. The current study indicated that both models contribute to our understanding of personality pathology, though conclusions were limited due to the size of the sample.

REFERENCES

American Psychiatric Association. (2000). Diagnostic and Statistical Manual of Mental Disorders, 4th ed., Text Revised. American Psychiatric Association, Washington DC.

American Psychiatric Association. (2011, June 21). *Personality disorders.* Retrieved June 2012, from http://www.dsm5.org/PROPOSEDRE VISIONS/Pages/PersonalityandPersonalityDisorders.aspx

American Psychiatric Association. (2012, May 1). Rationale for the proposed changes to the personality disorders classification in DSM-5. Retrieved June 2012, from http://www.dsm5.org/proposedrevision/Pages/ PersonalityDisorders.aspx

Artistico, D., Baldassarri, F., Lauriola, M., & Laicardi, C. (2000). Dimensions of health-related dispositions in elderly people: Relationships with health behavior and personality traits. *European Journal of Personality, 14,* 533-552.

Ashton, M. C., & Lee, K. (2001). A theoretical basis for the major dimensions of personality. *European Journal of Personality, 15,* 327-353.

Bagby, R. M., Sellbom, M., Costa, P. T., & Widiger, T. A. (2008). Predicting Diagnostic and Statistical Manual of Mental Disorders-IV personality disorders with the five-factor model of personality and the personality psychopathology five. *Personality and Mental Health, 2,* 55-69.

Bernstein, D. P., Iscan, C., & Maser, J. (2007). Opinions of personality disorder experts regarding the DSM-IV personality disorder classification system. *Journal of Personality Disorders, 32,* 536-551.

Block, J. (1995). A contrarian view of the five-factor approach to personality description. *Psychological Bulletin, 117,* 187-215.

Butcher, J. N., Dahlstrom, J. R., Graham, J. R., Tellegen, A., & Kaemmer, B. (1989). *Minnesota Multiphasic Personality Inventory-2 (MMPI-2). Manual for administration and scoring.* Minneapolis: University of Minnesota Press.

Butcher, J. N., Graham, J. R., Ben-Porath, Y. S., Tellegen, A., Dahlstrom, W. G., & Kaemmer, B. (2001). *MMPI-2 manual for administration scoring and interpretation, revised edition.* Minneapolis: University of Minnesota Press.

Clark, L. A. (2007). Assessment and diagnosis of personality disorder: Perennial issues and emerging conceptualization. *Annual Review of Psychology, 58,* 227-258.

Costa, P. T., & McCrae, R. R. (1992). *Revised NEO Personality Inventory (NEO PI-R) and NEO Five-Factor Inventory (NEO-FFI) professional manual.* Odessa, FL: Psychological Assessment Resources.

Costa, P. T., & McCrae, R. R. (1995). Domain and facets: Hierarchical personality assessment using the Revised NEO Personality Inventory. *Journal of Personality Assessment, 64*, 21-50.

Costa, P. T., McCrae, R. R., & Siegler, I. C. (1999). Continuity and change over the adult life cycle: Personality and personality disorders. In C. R. Cloninger (Eds.), Personality and Psychopathology (pp. 129-154). Arlington, VA: American Psychiatric Press, Inc.

Costa, P. T., & Widiger, T. A. (1994). Personality and personality disorders. *Journal of Abnormal Psychology, 103*, 78-91.

Costa, P. T., & Widiger, T. A. (2002). Personality disorders and the five-factor model of personality (2nd ed.). Washington, DC, US: American Psychological Association.

Digman, J. M., (1990). Personality structure: Emergence of the five-factor model. *Annual Review of Psychology, 41,* 417-440.

Eggers, J. I. M., Derksen, J. J., L., & DeMey, H. M. R. (1997). *Validation of MMPI-2 scales and profiles in outpatient and inpatient settings.* Paper presented at the 32nd Annual Symposium on Recent Developments in the Use of the MMPI-2 and MMPI-A, Minneapolis, MN.

First, M. B., Bell, C. C., Cuthbert, B., Krystal, J. H., Malison, R., Offord, D. R., Reiss, D., … Wisner, K. L. (2002). *Personality disorders and relational disorders: A research agenda for addressing crucial gaps in DSM.* In D. J. Kupfer, M. B. First, & D. A. Regier (Eds.), A Research Agenda for DSM-V. Arlington, VA: American Psychiatric Association.

First, M B., Gibbon, M., Spitzer, R. L., Williams, J. B. W., & Benjamin, L. S. (1997). *SCID-II personality questionnaire.* Washington, DC: American Psychiatric Press.

Haigler, E. D., & Widiger, T. A. (2001). Experimental manipulation of NEO-PI-R items. *Journal of Personality Assessment, 77*, 339-358.

Harkness, A. R. (1992). Fundamental topics in the personality disorders: Candidate trait dimensions from lower regions of the hierarchy. *Psychological Assessment, 4*, 251-259.

Harkness, A. R., Finn, J. A., McNulty, J. L., & Shields, S. M. (2011). The personality psychopathology-five (PSY-5): Recent constructive replication and assessment literature review. *Psychological Assessment, 24,* 432-443.

Harkness, A. R., & McNulty, J. L. (1994). The personality psychopathology five (PSY-5): Issue from the pages of a diagnostic manual instead of a dictionary. In S. Strack, & M. Lorr, *Differentiating normal and abnormal personality* (pp. 291-315). New York: Springer.

Harkness, A. R., McNulty, J. L., & Ben-Porath, Y. S. (1995). The personality psychopathology five (PSY-5): Construct and MMPI-2 scales. *Psychological Assessment, 7,* 104-114.

Hogan, J., & Holland B. (2003). Using theory to evaluate personality and job-performance relations: A socioanalytic perspective. *Journal of Applied Psychology, 88,* 100-112.

Jang, K. L., McCrae, R. R., Angleitner, A., Riemann, R., & Livesley, W. J. (1998). Heritability of Facet-level traits in a cross-cultural twin sample: Support for a hierarchical model of personality. *Journal of Personality and social Psychology, 74,* 1556-1565.

John, O. P., & Srivastava, S. (1999). The big five trait taxonomy: History, measurement, and theoretical perspectives. In L. A. Pervin & O. P. John (Eds.), Handbook of personality: Theory and research, (2nd ed., pp. 102-138). New York: The Guilford Press.

Krueger, R. F., Eaton, N. R., Clark, L. A., Watson, D., Markon, K. E., Derringer, J., … Livesley, W. J. (2011). Deriving an empirical structure of personality pathology for DSM-5. *Journal of Personality Disorders, 25,* 170-191.

Livesley, W. J. (2003). Diagnostic dilemmas in classifying personality disorder. In K. A. Phillips, M. B. First, & H. A. Pincus (Eds.), *Advancing DSM: Dilemmas in Psychiatric Diagnosis.* Washington, DC: American Psychiatric Association.

Loehlin, J. C., McCrae, R. R., Costa, P. T., & John, O. P. (1998). Heritabilities of common and measure-specific components of the big five personality factors. *Journal of Research in Personality, 32,* 431-453.

Marin-Avellan, L. E., McGauley, G., Campbell, C., & Fonagy, P. (2005). Using the SWAP-200 in a personality-disordered forensic population: Is it valid, reliable, and useful? *Criminal Behavior and Mental Health, 15,* 28-45.

McCrae, R. R., & Allik, J. (2002). *The five-factor model of personality across cultures.* New York, NY: Kluwer Academic/Plenum Publishers

McCrae, R. R., & Costa, P. T. (2003). *Personality in adulthood: A five-factor theory perspective.* New York, NY: The Guilford Press.

McCrae, R. R., Stone, S. V., Fagan, P. J., & Costa, P. T. (1998). Identifying causes of disagreement between self-reports and spouse ratings of personality. *Journal of Personality, 66,* 285-313.

McNulty, J. L., Ben-Porath, Y. S., & Watt, M. (1997). *Predicting SCID-II personality disorder symptomology: A comparison of the PSY-5 and Big Five models.* Paper presented at the 32nd Annual Symposium on Recent

Developments in the Use of the MMPI-2 and MMPI-A, Minneapolis, MN.

McNulty, J. L., Harkness, A. R., & Ben-Porath, Y. S. (1998). *Theoretical assertions and empirical evidence: How the MMPI-2 PSY-5 scales are linked with the MPQ, ZKPQ-III, and NEO-PI-R.* Paper presented at the 33rd Annual Symposium on Recent Developments in the Use of the MMPI-2 and MMPI-A, Clearwater Beach, FL.

Mullins-Sweatt, S. N., & Widiger, T. A. (2007). The Shedler and Westen assessment procedure from the perspective of general personality structure. *Journal of Abnormal Psychology, 116*, 618-623.

Quilty, L C., & Bagby, R. M. (2007). Psychometric and structural analysis of the MMPI-2 Personality Psychopathology Five (PSY-5) facet subscales. *Assessment, 14*, 375-384.

Rouse, S. V. (1997). The construct validity of the MMPI-2 PSY-5 scales in a clinical setting. Unpublished doctoral dissertation, University of Minnesota, Minneapolis.

Rouse, S. V., Butcher, J. N., & Miller, K. B. (1997). *Assessment of substance abuse problems in a sample of psychotherapy patients.* Paper presented at the 32nd Annual Symposium on Recent Developments in the Use of the MMPI-2 and MMPI-A, Minneapolis, MN.

Saulsman, L. M., & Page, A. C. (2005). The five-factor model and personality disorder empirical literature: A meta-analytic review. *Clinical Psychology Review, 23*, 1055-1085.

Shedler, J., & Westen, D. (2004). Refining DSM-IV personality disorder diagnosis: Integrating science and practice. *American Journal of Psychiatry, 161*, 1350-1365.

Shiner, R. L. (1998). How shall we speak of children's personalities in middle childhood? A preliminary taxonomy. *Psychological Bulletin, 124*, 308-332.

Tellegen, A. (1982). Brief manual for the Differential Personality Questionnaire. Unpublished manuscript, University of Minnesota, Minneapolis.

Tellegen, A., & Waller, N. G. (2008). Exploring personality through test construction: Development of the multidimensional personality questionnaire. In G. J. Boyle, G. Matthews., & D. H. Saklofske (Eds.), The SAGE handbook of personality theory and assessment, Vol 2: Personality measurement and testing. Thousand Oaks, CA, US: Sage Publications, Inc.

Thomas, K. M., Yalch, M. M., Krueger, R. F., Wright, A. G. C., Markon, K. E. & Hopwood, C. J. (in press). The convergent structure of DSM-5 personality trait facets and Five-Factor Model trait domains. *Assessment.*

Trull, T. J., & Durrett, C. A. (2005). Categorical and dimensional models of personality disorder. *Annual Review of Clinical Psychology, 1*, 355-380.

Trull, T. J., Useda, J. D., Costa, P. T., & McCrae, R. R. (1995). Comparison of the MMPI-2 personality psychopathology five (PSY-5), the NEO-PI, and the NEO-PI-R. *Psychological Assessment, 7*, 508-516.

Westen D. (1995). A clinical-empirical model of personality: Life after the Mischelian ice age and the NEO-lithic era. *Journal of Personality, 63*, 495-524.

Westen, D., & Muderrisoglu, S. (2003). Assessing personality disorders using a systematic clinical interview: Evaluation of an alternative to structured interviews. *Journal of Personality Disorders, 17*, 351-369.

Westen, D., & Muderrisoglu, S. (2006). Clinical assessment of pathological personality traits. *American Journal of Psychiatry, 163*, 1285-1287.

Widiger, T. A., & Mullins-Sweatt, S. N. (2005). Categorical and dimensional models of personality disorders. In J. M. Oldham, A. E. Skodol, & D. S. Bender (Eds.), The American Psychiatric Publishing textbook of personality disorders, Arlington, VA: American Psychiatric Publishing, Inc.

Widiger, T. A., & Simonsen, E. (2005). Alternative dimensional models of personality disorder: Finding a common ground. *Journal of Personality Disorders, 19*, 110-130.

Widiger, T. A., & Trull, T. J. (2007). Plate tectonics in the classification of personality disorder: Shifting to a dimensional model. *American Psychologist, 62*, 71-83.

Wright, A. G. C., Thomas, K. M., Hopwood, C. J., Markon, K. E., Pincus, A. L., & Krueger, R. F. (2012, March 26). The hierarchical structure of DSM-5 pathological personality traits. *Journal of Abnormal Psychology.* Advance online publication. doi: 10.1037/a0027669.

In: New Developments in Personality ...   ISBN: 978-1-62417-118-5
Editors: A. Morel and M. Durand   © 2013 Nova Science Publishers, Inc.

Chapter 3

FORENSIC AND NON-FORENSIC MENTAL HEALTH NURSES' APPROACH TO PERSONALITY/PSYCHOPATHIC DISORDERS: 'CLINICAL' VERSUS 'MANAGEMENT' PERSPECTIVES

Matt Bowen and Tom Mason[*]

University of Chester, Faculty of Health and Social Care,
Riverside, Castle Drive, Chester, England

ABSTRACT

The aim of this study was to compare forensic and non-forensic mental health nurses' perceptions in relation to their clinical or management focus for those with a diagnostic label of personality/psychopathic disorder. The method employed was a postal survey with the distribution of 1490 information gathering schedules across the UK with a response rate of 41.9% of forensic mental health nurses and 76.4% non-forensic mental health nurses being achieved. The results indicate that both groups saw these diagnostic labels more in terms of a management focus ($z = -3.79$; $p<0.01$) rather than a clinical one ($z = -3.53$; $p<0.01$) and that the forensic group scored higher on the management measure ($z = -17.31$; $p<0.01$) in relation to the non-

---

[*] Deceased, Professor.

forensic nurses ($z = -11.19$; $p<0.01$). The implications for practice are that nurses who focus more on a management perspective are less likely to facilitate therapeutic change with service users.

INTRODUCTION

People with a diagnosis of personality disorder have typically experienced adverse factors in childhood (Coid, 1999), including invalidating environments (Linehan, 1993) and often sexual and physical abuse (Lieb et al, 2004). Throughout adolescence and adulthood this group commonly experience the world as a persecutory environment in which they are unable to trust the motives of others (Bateman & Fonagy, 2004), are highly sensitized to being slighted leading to anger and aggression (APA, 2000), or feel crushed by self-punishment (Linehan et al. 2006). A review of services in the UK (NIMHE, 2003a), however, indicated that these interpersonal difficulties have often been compounded by services whose management approach has repeatedly led to excluding this group of people, rather than therapeutically engaging to facilitated change.

There have been a number of changes in the UK with regards the provision of services to people with a diagnosis of personality disorder. Within forensic psychiatry, the most notable change has been the development of services for a group identified as dangerous and severely personality disordered [D.S.P.D] (H.O. & D.oH., 1999). Within mainstream psychiatry there has been a move towards community based specialist services and the development of national guidelines for all mental health clinicians (NIMHE 2003b; NICE 2009a; NICE 2009b).

Changes to the Mental Health Act (1983) in the UK, has also meant that personality disorder is no longer distinguished from other mental disorders with regards the application to detain. In the 1983 Mental Health Act decisions to detain people with a diagnosis of personality disorder were informed by the belief that treatment was "likely to alleviate or prevent a deterioration of his condition" (DoH, 1983, S3(2)(b)) – commonly referred to as the 'treatability test'. In the absence of robust clinical evidence, this placed considerable significance on the beliefs of clinicians in the efficacy of treatments. The amendments to the Mental Health Act (2007) removed the treatability test and replaced it with the guidance that 'appropriate medical treatment is to be available for him' (DoH, 2007, S3(2)(d)). This has laid the way to increase inclusion of personality disorders within mainstream psychiatric provision, however, it remains unclear whether the removal of the treatability test has changed clinicians' beliefs about the clinical approach towards this group.

This paper reports on the results of a research project that explored the attitude and approach of forensic and non-forensic mental health nurses towards people with personality/psychopathic disorders with regards a management or a clinical perspective.

USE OF TERMS

In the UK the term forensic mental health nurse refers to nursing within services that exclusively provide treatment and care to mentally disordered offenders. These services are provided in three categories: high, medium and low security. High security services are provided exclusively through the National Health Service (N.H.S.) by three hospitals (Ashworth, Rampton and Broadmoor) for individuals who are considered to be a "grave and immediate danger to the public" (MHA, 1983). There are approximately 800 beds within High security hospitals. Medium security services are provided by a mixture of NHS and independent sector provision for people considered to "pose a serious danger to the public" (MHA, 1983), there are approximately 3,500 beds within this sector (Rutherford & Duggan, 2007).

Psychopathic disorder stems from the clinical developments of nineteenth and early twentieth century clinicians in England and Germany (Blackburn, 1993). Within the field of forensic psychiatry the term psychopathy, as developed by Cleckley (1976) and then later systematised by Hare (1991) has been regularly used as a psychological construct and the basis of research (Blackburn, 2000). Blackburn comments that in clinical practice psychopathic disorder is commonly regarded as a personality disorder (Blackburn, 2007). However, whilst there is some overlap of psychopathic disorder with the diagnostic category of antisocial personality disorder (APA, 2000) research suggests that the latter includes a broader clinical group (Hare, 1996). Kirkman (2008) has argued that this is a result of the greater conflation of personality traits and deviant behaviour within the criterion of antisocial personality disorder than in psychopathy.

The term psychopathic disorder is in common usage within forensic services in Britain (Blackburn, 2007), hence this research enquired about clinicians' experiences of psychopathic disorder and personality disorder in an attempt to reflect the clinical realities of the practitioners who were part of the research project. However, throughout this article the authors will use the diagnostic category personality disorder.

LITERATURE REVIEW

The literature in this field relates to nursing attitudes towards people with a diagnosis of personality disorder. Research in this area has tended to either adopt an approach of reviewing clinicians' attitudes towards the broad category of personality disorder, or specifically the attitudes of nurses towards people with a diagnosis of borderline personality disorder. The latter, no doubt, reflects the relatively high incidence of this clinical group within mainstream psychiatric services (APA, 2000) and whilst its focus is more specific than the research reported here an awareness of this body of work is instructive.

In the UK research into the attitudes of clinicians towards personality disordered clients can helpfully be seen in the context of Lewis and Appleby's seminal paper: "Personality Disorder: The patients psychiatrists dislike" (1988). The results of their research into the attitude and management responses of psychiatrists towards clinical vignettes, in which the inclusion or exclusion of a diagnosis of personality disorder was an independent variable, led them to conclude that the term personality disorder "appears to be an enduring pejorative judgement rather than a clinical diagnosis" (1988, p44).

As noted earlier, in the UK, the development of services to treat and care for people identified as having a dangerous and severe personality disorder has significantly changed the landscape of forensic psychiatric nursing to this client group. To support the development of these services within High Security Hospitals Len Bowers (2002) led a research project to explore the attitudes of nurses within the 3 High Security Hospitals, with the express intention of determining what could support nurses to retain a positive attitude in this area of work. His work indicated that only a small proportion of nurses considered this group to present few difficulties (less than 10%) and few nurses expressed optimism about treatment outcomes (less than 20%). The picture was not entirely bleak as there was a significant group of nurses who retained a positive attitude, which was reflected in their wish to engage therapeutically with the clients, and typically holding a belief that change was possible. Staff who worked in specific units for this client group were more likely to hold a positive attitude (though 14% believed none of the clients were treatable). Across the board there was a common experience of nurses responding to feeling let down by a service user, whose apparent progress seemed to unravel, with the majority of nurses deciding that this indicated that no one with this diagnosis should be trusted but a significant minority able to retain a positive but realistic attitude.

The above project evolved into an exploration of the attitudes of staff once the DSPD projects had been established, and a comparison of the attitudes of nurses and prison officers (Carr-Walker, Bowers, Callaghan, Nijman & Paton, 2004). Contrasting the attitudes of prison officers with the results already gained from the nurses within the High Security Hospitals, indicated that the prison officers were more positive in their attitude. Further analysis demonstrated that this related significantly to the method of recruitment to the services, as the prison officers had self-selected to work within the DSPD unit and their results were comparable to the minority of nurses who had self-selected to work on a personality disorder unit.

These projects led to the validation of the Attitude to Personality Disorder Questionnaire (Bowers & Allen, 2006) which is structured around five affective components: enjoyment/loathing; security/vulnerability; acceptance/rejection; purpose/futility; enthusiasm/exhaustion. This questionnaire has been used outside of the forensic environment to examine the attitudes of clinicians within a triage service (Purves & Sands, 2009). These results did indicate that the majority of nurses held a negative attitude but a significant minority held a positive attitude (47.4%). The component that the largest proportion of nurses scored negatively on was enjoyment/loathing (65% expressed loathing towards the client group) which the authors suggest reflects the tension of a profession which has caring as a cornerstone of its practices, working with a client group that is often characterised by struggles to accept and patterns of rejecting care.

Research by Newton-Howes, Weaver & Tyrer (2008) in a community mental health team into nurses' attitudes towards the broad diagnostic group of personality disorder, indicated that the inclusion of the diagnosis of personality disorder was positively associated with clinicians regarding the client are more chaotic, more aggressive and harder to manage.

There have been a number of research projects that have looked more specifically at the attitudes of non-forensic mental health nurses towards people with a diagnosis of borderline personality disorder. Cleary, Siegfried and Walter (2002) constructed a 23 item questionnaire to explore the experience, knowledge and attitudes of mental health staff in New South Wales with results indicating that 84% of staff felt this group was harder to work with than other clients. A modified version of the questionnaire was later used by James and Cowman (2007) who attained a similar response - 80% of nurses felt this was the hardest group to work with.

There has been some exploration about the attributes that nurses give to people with a diagnosis of borderline personality disorder to better understand the difficulties that nurses report experiencing. A significant factor has been identified as the degree of control that the nurse attributes to the client. Markham and Trower's (2003) research indicated that a diagnosis of borderline personality disorder was associated with the clients being attributed as having a greater control over their actions and nurses being less sympathetic in their responses. Nurses indicated that they considered this group to be more dangerous and were therefore themselves more socially distancing (Markham, 2003). This is consistent with Deans and Meocevic's (2006) research that indicated that 89% of nurses considered this group to be manipulative (i.e. that they had considerable control over their actions) and Forsyth's (2007) research that nurses' belief that the clients can control their actions was positively associated with nurses experiencing a high level of anger towards the service user.

The attitudes of staff have also been elicited indirectly through research that has examined the practice of clinicians working with people with a diagnosis of borderline personality disorder all of which have created datasets through in-depth interviews. Bergman and Eckerdal (2000) indicated the need for staff to retain an empathetic response to the clients, and the importance of them having an interest in the work. Langley and Klopper (2005) highlighted the importance of an attitude of trust and an approach of negotiated shared responsibility. Bowen's (2012) research highlighted the importance of staff retaining a compassionate attitude that enabled a rounded perception of the service user. These three research reports draw on a Winnicottian model of containment to understand the nurse's role in managing the strong emotions that the clients experience and the clinician's struggle to hold and make use of these emotions. Ma, Shih, Hsiao, Shih and Hayter (2009) identified a similar process to that indicated by Bowers (2002) in which the nurses had to manage an experience of the 'honeymoon period' coming to an end when the apparent good work appears to unravel. A capacity to retain a positive attitude after this experience was positively associated with better outcomes for these clients.

DEFINITION OF TERMS

The starting point in this research is to distinguish between the nurses having a 'clinical' or 'management' attitude towards patients with this diagnosis. 'Clinical' refers to those nurses who have an attitude of longer-term therapeutic optimism towards those with a personality disorder label whilst 'management' refers to those nurses who are more therapeutically pessimistic and tend towards short-term day-to-day supervision. Forensic mental health nurses are defined as 'those nurses working in secure psychiatric settings' whilst non-forensic mental health nurses are 'those nurses who work in general psychiatric facilities'.

THE RESEARCH QUESTIONS

The literature into the attitude and approach taken by nurses towards people with a diagnosis of personality disorders indicates that that the majority of nurses have a negative rather than a positive approach. This has been indicated to be the case across a range of forensic and non-forensic settings, and in response to both a general enquiry into attitudes to personality disorder and specifically borderline personality disorder. There has not, however, been research to specifically explore if there is a difference between the approaches of forensic and non-forensic nurses to this client group.

This led to the following research questions:

1) Do mental health nurses perceive people with a diagnostic label of personality disorder in 'management' terms to a greater extent than 'clinical' terms?
2) Are there differences in these perceptions between forensic mental health nurses and non-forensic mental health nurses?
3) If so, are these differences statistically significant?

METHOD

The method employed was a survey of forensic and non-forensic mental health nurses working across secure and non-secure psychiatric services in the UK. The secure psychiatric services involved high, medium and low settings as well as prison based mental health nurses and community outreach services for forensic clients.

Data Collection

An Information Gathering Schedule (IGS) was used which comprised of a scale pertaining to a clinical (Personality Disorder Clinical [PDC]) focus or a management (Personality Disorder Management [PDM]) focus relating to personality disordered patients. The IGS also contained demographic details and room for written commentary. The PDC-PDM binary theme was constructed from a number of questions and statements that were put before a panel of 15 forensic mental health nurses across a range of secure and non-secure psychiatric services. These panel members were asked to rank order the questions/statements as to their relevancy to each pole on the PDC and PDM theme. The criteria for inclusion on the 'clinical' pole was a major focus on therapeutic optimism (e.g. improvement, treatment outcomes, therapeutic approach) and for inclusion on the 'management' pole were absence of therapeutic optimism and a focus on day-to-day management (e.g. manipulation, splitting, crossing boundaries). The relevancy was ranked on a 1-11 point scale and the medians for each question/statement were computed to establish interquartile range. The Q value, or co-efficient of ambiguity, was 2-3 and the questions/statements were selected on this criteria. The remaining statements were eliminated and the test for relevancy was conducted by plotting the responses to each question/statement against all other statements. Twenty questions/statements pertaining to the clinical-management theme were then coded, scrambled and placed within the IGS. An example of the items include: 'Nurses believe that someone who is glib causes disruption to the ward' and 'Nurses view patients with a lack of remorse as relatively easy to treat'. These were scored on a 7-point Likert Scale from strongly agree to strongly disagree. This was piloted at a national conference of forensic mental health nurses with 100 IGSs distributed with a response rate of 78% being achieved. Following analysis several amendments were made and the IGS was then given to 20 forensic mental health nurses, the same group, on two occasions, 2 months apart to estimate reliability co-efficient which ranged from 0.7-0.9.

Sample

The sample inclusion criteria included mental health nurses in clinical practice with over two years of experience (this length of time was felt to be required to establish a degree of optimism/pessimism) and having nursed people with a diagnosis of personality disorder. The exclusion criteria included non-clinically based mental health nurses, nurse managers, nurse educators and no experience of nursing this patient group. From the Forensic Directory Website the total number of forensic units was obtained with an estimation of the total number of forensic mental health nurses established. In total the IGS was distributed to 1490 mental health nurses via a number of means dependent upon the requirement of the individual unit concerned. For example, on some sites a Lead person from the organisation distributed the questionnaire whilst at others a distribution list was given to the researchers to distribute themselves.

Data Management and Analysis

The data from the returned schedules were placed on a computer in Microsoft Excell and the Statistical Package for the Social Sciences (SPSS) version 17 for analysis. The analysis involved tabulation of data for frequencies, percentages and prevalence, tests for normality using the Kolmogorov-Smirnov test, the Mann-Whitney for comparing the ranked scores and the Wilcoxon test on the paired samples.

Ethical Considerations

Ethical approval was sought and obtained from the Multi-site Research Ethics Committee and from each of the individual sites. Voluntary status was achieved through non-response by declining to complete or return the questionnaire and confidentiality maintained through no personal identifying data being requested. The data were placed on computer under password within a locked room in a university setting. No raw data were transported elsewhere.

RESULTS

A ten per cent sample of forensic mental health nurses from high and medium secure services and general mental health services, and a fifty per cent sample from low, prison and community forensic services formed the sampling frame and these can be seen in Table 1.

Table 1. Sample numbers and response rates

Forensic Settings	Sample	Response Rate % and N=	Non-Forensic Settings	Sample	Response Rate % and N=
High	400	(33.5) 134	General	500	(76.4) 382
Medium	320	(38.1) 122			
Low	120	(56.6) 68			
Prison	50	(66) 33			
Community	100	(58) 58			
Totals	990	(41.9) 415		500	(76.4) 382

The response rates can also be seen in table one. The response rate of the non-forensic nurses was significantly better than the forensic nurses. This meant that the number of returned questionnaires between the two groups was closer, in quantity, than the number distributed. The demographic details can be seen in Table 2. It can be seen from table two that there were more male respondents than females across all groups. The difference in gender weighting was particularly marked among the forensic nurses, with High and Medium secure environments having more than twice the proportion of males to female respondents. The RMN (Registered Mental Nurse) qualification was the most common qualification across all areas. With regards length of clinical experience, the non-forensic nurses were very heavily weighted in the medium lengths i.e. between 6 – 15 years. By contrast the forensic nurses, particularly the High and Medium Security environments had a more even distribution across the range of years of experience. The nurses' grades were very heavily weighted in the three middle bands E-G, this was the case across the different clinical environments.

Table 2. Demographic details of the sample

	High	Medium	Low	Prison	Community	General	Totals
Gender							
Male	93	87	41	21	32	201	475
Female	41	35	27	12	26	181	322
	134	122	68	33	58	382	
Qualifications							
RMN	69	78	41	21	39	272	520
RMN/RGN	6	18	4	6	9	24	67
RMN/RNMH	10	8	6	2	6	26	58
RMN/EN	15	10	9	0	4	12	38
RNMH	34	8	8	4	0	48	54
	134	122	68	33	58	382	
Forensic Experience							
2-5	27	38	26	11	17	86	205
6-10	39	51	20	17	23	155	305
11-15	42	21	14	5	14	110	206
>16	26	12	8	0	4	31	81
	134	122	68	33	58	382	
Nursing Grade							
D	19	17	8	0	4	48	96
E	45	33	18	12	18	76	202
F	43	46	19	14	16	144	282
G	21	14	20	7	16	98	176
H	6	12	3	0	4	16	41
	134	122	68	33	58	382	

RMN – Registered Mental Nurse.

RGN – Registered General Nurse.

EN – Enrolled Nurse.

RNMH – Registered Nurse Mental Health.

Nursing Grades. Post Qualification grades in nursing started at Grade D and rose to Grade I.

All scores for both Forensic and Non-Forensic groups were non-normal in relation to PDC (10; 6; 8 and 12; 7; 8 respectively) and PDM (21; 7; 24 and 19; 7; 20 respectively).

Results from the independent samples Mann-Whitney tests show statistically significant differences between Forensic and Non-Forensic groups on ranked scores from the PDC measure ($z = -0.53$; $p<0.01$) and the PDM measure ($z = -3.79$; $p<0.01$). This suggests that both these groups scored higher on the management scale as opposed to the clinical measure, which indicates that they perceived personality disordered patients more in terms of managing their behaviour rather than therapeutically engaging them.

The results from the paired samples Wilcoxon tests show statistically significant differences between ranked scores on the PDC-PDM measures from the Forensic group ($z = -17.31$; $p<0.01$) and the Non-Forensic group ($z = -11.19$; $p<0.01$). These figures suggest that the Forensic group saw the management of these diagnostic labels to a greater extent than did the Non-Forensic group of mental health nurses. These results can be graphically displayed in a bar chart format (see Figures 1 and 2).

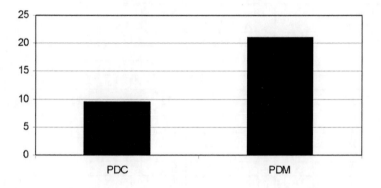

Figure 1. Forensic Nurses PDC-PDM measures.

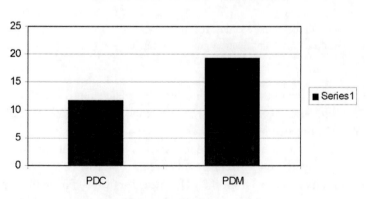

Figure 2. Non-Forensic Nurses PDC-PDM measures.

DISCUSSION

The research data indicates that both forensic and non-forensic clinicians are more inclined to view personality disordered individuals in terms of a 'management' rather a 'clinical' approach.

It is assumed that the level of severity of the clients would tend to be greater in the forensic services so this might be reflected in a greater tendency towards a management approach in forensic services than non-forensic services. Research by Bowers (2002) also indicated that nurses in High Security Hospitals believed that some management decisions were made because of fear of a media reaction to the treatment of high profile service users. With the well documented heightened preoccupation with risk in mental health services (Manning, 2002) as well as high profile examples of personality disordered individuals generating unwelcome media attention (e.g. Michael Stone in the UK and John Hinkley in the US), this would exert a strong pressure to be more pre-occupied with management as a way of protecting individual staff and the institution's reputation.

Whilst the responses between the forensic and non-forensic nurses are statistically different and therefore warrant some consideration there are strong similarities between the two groups of nurses. As the two groups were responding to the same IGS this suggests that there are similarities across settings in problems that arise that encourage a management approach in nursing personality disordered clients.

Some writers have drawn on a Winnicotian concept of containment (Bergman and Eckerdal 2000; Langley and Klopper 2005; Bowen 2012) to explore what they consider to be a vital role of the nurse with this client group. Namely, to be able to withstand making contact with the strong and rapidly changing emotional world of the clients and for the nurse to use that to make sense of the situation and ultimately for the client to have a better understanding of themselves. Adoption of a management approach could be seen as a breakdown in the nurse's capacity to contain the strong emotions of the clients, and their own emotional reaction. Unfortunately, because the concept of containment is borne out of a psychoanalytic model it raises doubts in some minds about whether or not it is applicable to mental health nurses more generally, and in environments that do not use a psychodynamic approach.

An alternative model for thinking about the use of a management rather than a clinical approach to the work is that it is a break down in the empathetic link between the nurse and the client. By retaining an empathetic link with the client the nurse is able to develop a rounded picture of the service user: why they are in their current situation, why they respond to their environment as they do, what their strengths are, what their fears are, etc. By contrast a management approach which focusses on minimising the negative impact the service user has on others, with little interest in the person's internal world or hope of therapeutic change indicates a severance of an empathetic link.

The issue of empathy as central to staff gaining greater clinical competence has particular relevance when thinking about personality disorders. Robert Hare (1991), for example, considers lack of empathy as central to an understanding of psychopathy and Kernberg (1967) views a limited capacity to develop mature empathy as central to understanding the broad category of borderline personality organisation. Often the intensity of the rapidly changing emotional world of the personality disordered individual (Gunderson, 2009) seriously inhibits their ability to retain a consistent and rounded picture of other people (Bateman & Fonagy, 2004). As a consequence the capacity of this group to trust that they can empathetically link with others (Bowen, 2007) or to trust their own resources (Langley and Klopper 2005) is routinely undermined. If struggling to establish empathetic links with others is central to the disturbance that this client group experiences, then therapeutically working with this struggle will be central to the role of the mental health nurse.

Reports from staff working with the group is that they commonly feel disoriented as they realise that they are being related to as if they were someone else, often as a representation from the person's past, often as someone persecutory (Bowen, 2012). This type of experience is a familiar example of a limited capacity to create empathetic links with others that undermines the service user's ability to experience and receive care that is on offer. Failure to support the client to work with this struggle would then be most clearly indicated by the nurse's own struggle or inability to retain an empathetic link. That 65% of nurses are reported to experience loathing towards this group (Purves & Sands, 2009) does not simply reflect the challenge of a caring professional caring for people who reject care. It also reflects a professional relationship in which the client's disturbance in their ability to form empathetic links with others triggers an unempathetic reaction in the nurse. From this perspective, the predominantly management orientation of both forensic and non-forensic nurses is an expression of a failure to contain the clients' struggle to maintain empathy through adopting an unempathetic stance in the clinical work.

The advantage of placing empathy as a central concept is that it implies that the particular psychological model that is used to understand the clinical work is not of central importance.

It suggests that all models to help staff understand the links between an individual's biography and that person's capacity to understand the motives of others, trust their own emotional responses, and manage their fluctuating emotional states would be helpful.

There is some support for this model which places retaining an empathetic link with others as central to this work. Main's seminal work *The Ailment* (1989) for example, documents how a staff team working with particularly difficult clients damage their empathetic links with each other. Bergman and Eckerdal's (2000) research indicated that staff retaining an empathetic position towards the clients was vital for effective therapeutic work. Whereas Evans' (2007) account of providing clinical supervision to mental health nurses working with borderline personality disordered clients notes that the particular emotional strains of the work, had a tendency to undermine the nurses' capacity to retain an empathetic stance. Instead the nurses typically fell into one of two camps of viewing the service users in a partial rather than in a mature empathetic position either as: a victim, or as manipulative. Forsyth's (2007) research indicated that the greater the level of control attributed to the person's actions the lower the level of empathy the nurses felt, and research indicates that nurses typically attribute a high level of control to personality disordered clients (Bowers 2002; Markham & Trowers 2003). The central importance of establishing and retaining an empathetic position is emphasised by research by Krawitz (2004) and separately by Treloar and Lewis (2008) into the efficacy of training mental health nurses to work therapeutically with this group. Both projects identified the development of empathy by the participants towards these clients as the single strongest indicator of future therapeutic impact.

Mechanisms to support the development and retention of empathetic links between nurses and personality disordered clients would therefore include training that provides models for understanding the internal worlds of the clients, highlighting the importance of disturbacnce in the capacity for mature empathy.

Clinical supervision has also been indicated as helpful to maintain a thoughtful and empathetic approach to the work (Bowers, 2002). Mechanisms to identify disturbances in empathetic links between staff would also be important, drawing on Hinshelwood's (2001) account of how staff teams can learn from these disruptions.

LIMITATIONS

There are a number of limitations to this study. First, the postal survey design is limited in what type of data can be collected. Despite the space allowed for 'further comments' these sections were largely left uncompleted. Second, statistical approaches tend to leave the researchers with more questions than answers due to the need for further exploration and elucidation. A third limitation is the wide range of behaviours that constitute the 'clinical' conditions of personality disorders, which may distort the mental health nurses' perceptions, and further refinement and research is required to address this. Fourth is the different response rates between forensic and non-forensic nurses, this suggests that strategies should be developed to increase the response rates of forensic nurse.

CONCLUSION

The research established differences in the attitude and approach of forensic and non-forensic mental health nurses in a range of secure and non-secure psychiatric services. Both groups of mental health nurses saw personality disordered patients more in terms of 'management' rather than 'clinical' terms, with the forensic nursing group to a greater statistically significant level. The importance of these findings for practice is that if mental health nurses adopt a more 'negative' perception towards the 'management' of people with these disorders then the nursing care has only a limited chance of facilitating therapeutic change. There were strong similarities between the two nursing groups, who were responding to the same IGS across a wide range of services. This suggests that there are some common difficulties in nursing this client group, which is perhaps surprising given the very broad clinical presentations that the term "personality/ psychopathic disorders" encompasses, and the broad range of services involves. It has been suggested that a common difficulty that leads to a management approach is a disturbance in the empathetic link between staff and service users, which reflects a common struggle among this clinical group to establish mature empathetic links with other people. However, it should be borne in mind that the struggle to maintain an empathetic link by staff in different services, working with different types of clients, will present different challenges – e.g a service such as triage that predominantly works with people who self-harm, compared with a DSPD units where many people have committed violent offences against others. The results suggest that further research into the impact of the clinical work on staff's capacity to form empathetic links with others, particularly clients, but also other staff could help better understand the challenges to this aspect of clinical work.

ACKNOWLEDGMENT

Kat Melling. For assistance with statistical work.

REFERENCES

American Psychiatric Association (2000) *Diagnostic and Statistical Manual of Mental Disorders, 4th Edition, Text Revision.* Washington, DC: American Psychiatric Association.

Bateman, A. & Fonagy, P. (2004). Psychotherapy for Borderline Personality Disorder: Mentalization-based treatment. Oxford University Press, Oxford, UK.

Bergman, B., & Eckerdal, A. (2000). Professional skills and frame of work organization in managing borderline personality disorder: Shared philosophy or ambivalence – A qualitative study from the view of caregivers. *Scandinavian Journal of Caring Science*, 14: 245-252

Blackburn, R. (1993) *The Psychology of Criminal Conduct: Theory, Research and Practice.* Chichester: John Wiley & Sons.

Blackburn, R. (2000). Classification and assessment of personality disorders in mentally disordered offenders: a psychological perspective. *Criminal Behaviour and Mental Health*, 10: s8-s33

Blackburn, R. (2007). Personality disorder and psychopathy: conceptual and empirical integration. Psychology, Crime and Law, 13(1): 7-18.

Bowen, M. (2007). A Systems Approach to Understanding the Primary Task of the Henderson Hospital. Therapeutic Communities, 28(2): 137-147.

Bowen, M. (2012). Borderline Personality Disorder: clinicians' accounts of good practice. Journal of Psychiatric and Mental Health Nursing, *in press.*

Bowers, L (2002). Dangerous and Severe Personality Disorder. Response and Role of the Psychiatric Team. London: Routledge.

Bowers, L. & Allan, T. (2006). The attitudes to personality disorder questionnaire: Psychometric properties and results. *Journal of Personality Disorders*, 2(3): 281-293.

Carr-Walker, P., Bowers, L., Callaghan, P., Nijman, H. & Paton, J. (2004). Attitudes towards personality disorders: Comparison between prison officers and psychiatric nurses. *Legal and Criminological Psychology*, 9: 265–277.

Cleary M., Siegfield N. & Walters G. (2002). Experience, knowledge and attitudes of mental health staff regarding clients with a borderline personality disorder. International Journal of Mental Health Nursing 11, 186–191.

Cleckley, H. (1976) *The Mask of Insanity*. Fifth Edition. St. Louis: Mosby.

Coid J. (1999) Aetiological Risk Factors for Personality Disorders. British Journal of Psychiatry 174, 530–538.

Deans, C. & Meocevic, E (2006). Attitudes of registered psychiatric nurses towards patients diagnosed with borderline personality disorder. Contemporary Nurse, 21: 43-49.

Department of Health (1983) *The Mental Health Act 1983*. HMSO. London: UK.

Department of Health (2007). *The Mental Health Act 2007*. HMSO. London:uk.

Evans, M. (2007). Being driven mad: towards understanding borderline and other disturbed states of mind through the use of counter-transference. Psychoanalytic Psychotherapy, 21(3): 216-232.

Forsyth, A. (2007). The effects of diagnosis and non-compliance attributions on therapeutic alliance processes in adult acute psychiatric settings. Journal of Psychiatric and Mental Health Nursing, 14: 33–40.

Gunderson, J. G. (2009). Borderline Personality Disorder: Ontogeny of a Diagnosis. American Journal of Psychiatry, 166:530–539.

Hare, R.D. (1991). *Manual for the Hare Psychopathy Checklist – Revisited*. Toronto: Multi-Health Systems.

Hare, R. D. (1996). Psychopathy: A clinical construct whose time has come. Criminal Justice and Behaviour, 23(1), 25-54.

Hinshelwood, R. D. (2001) *Thinking About Institutions. Milieux and Madness*. London: Jessica Kingsley Publications.

Home Office & Department of Health (1999). *Managing dangerous people with severe personality disorder: proposals for policy development.* HMSO: London, UK.

James, P.D. & Cowman, S. (2007) Psychiatric nurses' knowledge, experience and attitudes towards clients with borderline personality disorder. *Journal of Psychiatric and Mental Health Nursing.* 14: 670-78.

Kernberg, O. (1967) Borderline personality organisation. *Journal of the American Psychoanalytic Association.* 15: 641-85.

Kirkman, C.A. (2008). Psychopathy: a confusing clinical construct. *Journal of Forensic Nursing.* 4: 29-39.

Krawitz, R. (2004). Borderline personality disorder: attitudinal change following training. *Australian and New Zealand Journal of Psychiatry.*38: 554-559.

Langley, G., C. &Klopper, H. (2005).Trust as a foundation for the therapeutic intervention for patients with borderline personality disorder. Journal of Psychiatric and Mental Health Nursing,12: 23–32.

Lewis, G. & Appleby, L. (1988). Personality Disorder: The Patients Psychiatrists Dislike *British Journal of Psychiatry*, 153: 44-49

Lieb, K., Zanarini,M. C., Schmahl,C., Linehan,M. M. and. Bohus,M. (2004). Borderline personality disorder. Lancet 364: 453-461.

Linehan, M. (1993). Cognitive Behavioural Treatment of Borderline Personality Disorder (Diagnosis & Treatment of Mental Disorders). Guildford Press. Guildford: UK.

Ma W.F., Shih F.J., Hsiao S.M., et al. (2009). 'Caring Across Thorns' – different care outcomes for borderline personality disorder patients in Taiwan. *Journal of Clinical Nursing* 18, 440–450.

Lineham, M.M., Comtois, K.A., Murray, A.M., Brown, M.Z., Gallop, R.J., Heard, H.L., Korslund, K.E., Tutek, D.A., Reynolds, S.K. &Lindenboim, N. (2006) Two-year randomized controlled trial and follow-up of dialectical behaviour therapy vs therapy by experts for suicidal behaviors and borderline personality disorder. Archives of General Psychiatry, 63 (7): 757-66.

Ma, W.F., Shih, F.J., Hsiao, S.M., Shih, S.N., Hayter, M (2009).'Caring Across Thorns'--different care outcomes for borderline personality disorder patients in Taiwan. Journal of Clinical Nursing, 18(3): 440-450.

Main, T. (1989) *The Ailment and Other Psychoanalytic Essays*. London: Free Association Books.

Manning, N. (2002) Actor networks, policy networks and personality disorder. *Sociology of Health and Illness.* 24(5): 644-66.

Markham, D. (2003) Attitudes towards patients with a diagnosis of 'borderline personality disorder': social rejection and dangerousness. *Journal of Mental Health.* 12 (6): 595-612.

Markham, D. & Trower, P. (2003) The effects of the psychiatric label 'borderline personality disorder' on nursing staff's perception and causal attributions for challenging behaviours. *British Journal of Clinical Psychology.* 42: 243-56.

N.I.C.E (2009a) *Borderline Personality Disorder: Treatment and Management.* London: DoH. N.I.C.E (2009b) *Antiosocial Personality Disorder: Treatment, Management and Prevention.* London: DoH.

NIMHE (2003a). Personality Disorder: No Longer a Diagnosis of Exclusion. NIMHE (2003b). Personality Disorder: Capability Framework.

Newton-Howes, G., Weaver, T. & Tyrer, P. (2008). Attitudes of staff towards patients with personality disorder in community mental health teams. *Australian and New Zealand Journal of Psychiatry*, 42:572-577

Purves, D. & Sands, N. (2009). Crisis and Triage Clinicians' Attitudes Toward Working With People With Personality Disorder. *Perspectives in Psychiatric Care*, 45(3): 208-215.

Rutherford, M. & Duggan, S. (2007). Forensic Mental Health Services. Facts and figures on current provision. Sainsbury Centre for Mental Health

Treloar ,A.J.C. & Lewis, A.J. (2008). Targeted clinical education for staff attitudes towards deliberate self-harm in borderline personality disorder: randomised controlled trial. *Australian and New Zealand Journal of Psychiatry.* 42: 981-988.

In: New Developments in Personality ...   ISBN: 978-1-62417-118-5
Editors: A. Morel and M. Durand   © 2013 Nova Science Publishers, Inc.

Chapter 4

THE MILLON CLINICAL MULTIAXIAL INVENTORY–III (MCMI-III) AND THE PERSONALITY DISORDER QUESTIONNAIRE-4+ (PDQ-4+) IN A MIXED ITALIAN PSYCHIATRIC SAMPLE

Gioia Bottesi[1], Caterina Novara[1], Marta Ghisi[1], Stefano Ferracuti[2], Margherita Lang[3], Ezio Sanavio[1] and Alessandro Zennaro[4]

[1]Department of General Psychology, University of Padova, Italy
[2]Department NESMOS,"Sapienza" University of Roma, Italy
[3]Department of Psychology, University of Milano-Bicocca, Italy
[4]Department of Psychology, University of Torino, Italy

ABSTRACT

Self-report questionnaires play a crucial role in the assessment of Personality Disorders (PDs); in such a context, the Millon Clinical Multiaxial Inventory–III (MCMI-III) and the Personality Disorder Questionnaire-4+ (PDQ-4+) are frequently adopted. The aim of this preliminary study was to examine the association between the MCMI-III and the PDQ-4+ in a mixed Italian psychiatric sample.

All the correlations between the MCMI-III personality scales and the correspondent PDQ-4+ scales were positive and generally good. The only exceptions were represented by the Histrionic and Narcissistic PDs. Strong associations between several MCMI-III clinical scales and PDQ-4+ personality scales also emerged.

The present data support the good correspondence between the Italian versions of MCMI-III and PDQ-4+. Nevertheless, further research on the Histrionic and Narcissistic scales is necessary. Recent literature, however, seems to support our findings.

Keywords: Millon Clinical Multiaxial Inventory–III; Personality Disorder Questionnaire-4+; personality disorders; assessment

INTRODUCTION

Widiger and Samuel (2005) proposed a two-step procedure for the assessment of Personality Disorders (PDs). The first step is a screening phase, in which it is useful to administer a short and simple questionnaire with the aim of reducing the number of potential diagnoses and direct the subsequent investigation. Consequently, in the second phase specific sections of semi-structured interviews have to be administered to verify the actual occurrence of the PD (Widiger and Samuel, 2005). Moreover, clinicians are often in disagreement when assessing the same patient, despite the Diagnostic and Statistic Manual of Mental Disorders – Fourth Edition- Text Revision (DSM-IV-TR; American Psychiatric Association, 2000) provides accurate and operational diagnostic criteria. Nonetheless, it is to note that DSM-IV-TR diagnostic criteria for PDs are currently under revision because of some critical points (Skodol and Bender, 2009) and, therefore, the absence of an agreement between clinicians might be attributable to issues concerning the criteria themselves. For these reasons, the role of self-report questionnaires is crucial in helping clinicians to identify the correct diagnosis: in clinical practice, the Millon Clinical Multiaxial Inventory–III (MCMI-III; Millon, Davis, and Millon, 1997) and the Personality Diagnostic Questionnaire-4+ (PDQ-4+; Hyler, 1994) are widely adopted instruments.

MCMI-III represents the revised version of the previous MCMI (Millon, 1983) and MCMI-II (Millon, 1987), developed according to both DSM criteria and Millon's evolutionary model of personality (Millon, 1996). Several authors pointed out its lack of discriminant validity (Boyle and Le Dean, 2000; Lindsay, Sankis, and Widiger, 2000), which is primarily ascribable to the over-diagnosis of PDs among clinical samples. On the other hand, it has been demonstrated MCMI's good specificity (Guthrie and Mobley, 1994; Kennedy et al., 1995; Marlowe, Husband, Bonieskie, Kirby, and Platt, 1997; Messina, Wish, Hoffman, and Nemes, 2001). The PDQ-4+ is the more recent revision of the two previous PDQ (Hyler, Rieder, Spitzer, and Williams, 1983) and PDQ-R (Hyler and Rieder, 1987) and was constructed to obtain a specific correspondence with DSM-IV-TR criteria. Several authors (Davison, Leese, and Taylor, 2001; Fossati et al., 1998; Wilberg, Dammen, and Friis, 2000) suggested that the total PDQ-4+ score might be suitable for screening for the presence of PDs, as it produces many false-positive PD diagnoses, whereas the false negative rates are very low. Therefore, PDQ-4+ may be useful in identifying patients who, being above the predicted cut-off, need to be further assessed; it cannot be considered, however, as a screening instrument for specific PDs.

The occurrence of false-positive assessments is fairly common among self-report inventories (Dubro, Wetzler, and Kahn, 1988; Hyler, Skodol, Oldham, Kellman, and Doidge, 1992). Nonetheless, it is to stress that self-report questionnaires are generally administered to guide the clinician during the assessment process rather than to establish definitive diagnoses. Thus, MCMI-III and PDQ-4+'s tendency to over-diagnose might be seen as a strength rather than a limitation: since it allows to identify a wider range of potential areas of interest, it leads to a deeper and more punctual investigation when administering semi-structured interviews. This is consistent with the procedure suggested by Widiger and Samuels (2005).

A few studies making use of previous versions of both MCMI and PDQ have been conducted, but only a scarce number aimed at investigating the association between them. For example, Reich and Troughton (1988) administered both the inventories to detect PDs among patients with panic disorder; Guthrie and Mobley (1994) performed a study to investigate the relative diagnostic efficiency of a series of personality questionnaires, including MCMI-II and PDQ-R, on an outpatient sample; Lindsay and Widiger (1995) administered only four scales (i.e. Histrionic, Dependent, Antisocial and Narcissistic) of both MCMI-II and PDQ-R, plus other self-report inventories, in order to detect gender biases. On the other hand, Blackburn, Donnelly, Logan and Renwick (2004) evaluated the association between MCMI-II and PDQ, finding good correlations for Avoidant, Schizoid and Antisocial PDs, but a poor one for Histrionic, Narcissistic and Obsessive-compulsive PDs.

To our knowledge, no previous study on the association between MCMI-III and PDQ-4+ has been performed. Indeed, only three studies were conducted using the more recent versions of both the inventories, but they offered limited information and investigated psychopathy and Antisocial PD (Hicklin and Widiger, 2005), gender bias in self-report PDs inventories (Lindsay et al., 2000) and reactions of lay, patient and professional groups to self-report inventories (Blount, Evans, Birch, Warren, and Norton, 2002).

The purpose of the present preliminary study is to examine the correspondences between MCMI-III and PDQ-4+ personality scales and the association between MCMI-III clinical scales and PDQ -4+ personality scales in a mixed Italian psychiatric sample.

METHOD

Participants

Fifty outpatients consecutively admitted to mental health centers in Central Italy; they received a DSM-IV-TR Axis I or Axis II diagnosis using the Structured Clinical Interviews for DSM-IV (First, Spitzer, Gibbon, and Williams, 1996; First, Spitzer, Gibbon, Williams, and Benjamin, 1996). Twenty-nine subjects were males (58%) and 21 were females (42%). The mean age was 39 years (SD = 11.4) and the mean years of education were 12.1 (SD = 3.7); as regards marital status, 54% of participants was single, 26% married, 6% separated, 8% divorced, 4% had a live-in partner and 2% was widowed. There were no significant differences between genders as regards age ($F_{(1,48)}$ = 1.919; p = .172), years of education ($F_{(1,48)}$ = .297; p = .588) and marital status ($\chi^2_{(5)}$ = 5.873; p = .319). The most frequent diagnosis was mood disorders (26 subjects); the remainder of the diagnoses included anxiety disorders (9 subjects), personality disorders (8 subjects), schizophrenia or other psychotic disorders (7 subjects).

Materials and Procedure

All the participants gave their written consent to participation in the study before filling in the two questionnaires. The two inventories were administered in counter-balanced order to avoid order effects.

MCMI-III. It is a 175-item self-report questionnaire in a true-false format, which identifies 14 pathological personality styles. It also provides 10 scales corresponding to as many clinical syndromes, and 4 indexes to assess validity and response styles: V (Validity), X (Disclosure), Y (Desirability), Z (Debasement). Raw scores have to be transformed in standard scores defined as "Base Rates" (BR), which are based on percentiles. The internal consistency of the original version is moderate, with Cronbach alpha values ranging from .66 to .95. The mean test-retest reliability (from 5 to 14 days) is characterized by values of r equal to or greater than .82 (except for the H-Somatoform scale, r = .96).

The original MCMI-III scales demonstrated good predictive power (indexes ranging from .30 to .81) and excellent sensitivity (values from .54 to .92; Millon et al., 1997). Convergent validity between the MCMI-III and the Minnesota Multiphasic Personality Inventory-2 (MMPI-2; Butcher, Dahlstrom, Graham, Tellegen, and Kraemmer, 1989) resulted good (Millon, 1997).

In the Italian version (Zennaro, Ferracuti, Lang, and Sanavio, 2008) the conversion of raw scores in BRs was shown not to be useful and not to increase validity when compared with the results obtained with raw scores. The convergent validity with the MMPI-2's scales resulted good (Zennaro et al., 2008) and in line with that reported by Millon and colleagues (1997). Data regarding predictive power of the Italian version revealed low validity of MCMI-III scales, whereas effect sizes have been found to be good in discriminating pathologic and healthy subjects: Cohen's *d* values are, in most scales, less than .30 and, in 6 scales, greater than .80 (Zennaro et al., 2008).

PDQ-4+. It requires subjects to answer each question thinking about what happened "during most of the last years". The inventory is composed of 99 items in a true-false format and is designed to measure the 10 PDs included in DSM-IV-TR and the 2 PDs (Negativistic and Depressive) reported in the DSM-IV-TR appendix. The mean internal consistency value of the 12 scales reported for Italian and Chinese clinical samples (Fossati et al., 1998; Yang et al., 2000) was .62 (range from .46 to .74). The test-retest reliability after 10 days was .67 (range from .48 to .79; Yang et al., 2000); after 15 days it was .87 (Kim, Choi and Cho, 2000). PDQ-4+ convergent validity has been tested with the SCID-II and the Longitudinal, Expert, All Data procedure (LEAD; Spitzer, 1983) as external diagnostic standards for PDs; results indicated a general poor diagnostic agreement between the two measures for specific PDs (Davison et al., 2001; Wilberg et al., 2000) As far as regards the Italian version, internal consistency reliability has been calculated in a sample of 300 Italian psychiatric patients; K-R values were low, ranging from .46 and .74. Concerning convergent validity, low correlations between the PDQ-4+ and the SCID-II emerged, ranging from r = .20 to r = .40 (Fossati, et al., 1998).

RESULTS

For both questionnaires raw scores were used.

Table 1 shows the correlation matrix for the MCMI-III personality scales and the PDQ-4+ scales. Most of the correlations between the MCMI-III personality scales and the corresponding PDQ-4+ scales resulted positive and good; several correspondences were particularly high, specifically those for Antisocial, Schizotypal and Dependent PDs. The only exceptions concerned the correlation between the Histrionic PD scales, which resulted negative and non significant, and the one between the two Narcissistic PD scales, which resulted very modest.

The correlations between the MCMI-III clinical scales and the PDQ-4+ personality scales are displayed in table 2. Worthy of note are the associations between the MCMI-III Anxiety, Dysthymia, Post Traumatic Stress, Thought Disorder and Major Depression clinical scales and the PDQ-4+ Depressive PD scale. Moreover, both the MCMI-III Alcohol Dependence and Drug Dependence clinical scales showed high correlations with the PDQ-4+ Antisocial PD scale, while only the MCMI-III Alcohol Dependence clinical scale resulted correlated with the PDQ-4+ Negativistic and Borderline PDs scales. Lastly, high correlations between the MCMI-III Anxiety, Bipolar:Manic, Dysthymia, Post Traumatic Stress, Thought Disorder and Delusional Disorder clinical scales and the PDQ-4+ Schizotypal PD scale emerged.

CONCLUSION

Present study examined the associations between the MCMI-III and the PDQ-4+ in a mixed Italian psychiatric sample; to our knowledge, it represents the first attempt to investigate the correspondence between the recent versions of these two self-report inventories.

The analysis of the correlations revealed excellent correspondences between the different PD scales. Moreover, the strong correlations emerged for the Antisocial and Schizotypal PDs are in line with results found by Blackburn and colleagues (2004), who made use of the MCMI-II and the PDQ-R.

Table 1. Correlations between the MCMI-III personality scales and the PDQ-4+ scales

MCMI-III scales	PDQ-4+ Scales											
	Schd	Avoid	Depr	Dep	Histr	Narc	Antis	Obses	Nega	Scht	Bord	Para
1 Schizoid	.58**	.59**	.53**	.38**	.30*	.29*	.28	-.03	.16	.58**	.38**	.11
2A Avoidant	.47**	.63**	.70**	.51**	.33*	.32*	.41**	.04	.38**	.58**	.41**	.24
2B Depressive	.50**	.75**	.77**	.48**	.41**	.29	.30*	.25	.48**	.59**	.40**	.25
3 Dependent	.41**	.77**	.79**	.68**	.42**	.31*	.36*	.24	.41**	.57**	.42**	.16
4 Histrionic	-.33*	-.55**	-.54**	-.35*	-.14	-.13	.07	-.03	-.25	-.37**	-.24	.02
5 Narcissistic	.09	-.37*	-.35*	-.19	.26	.28*	.26	.17	-.06	-.02	.05	.28*
6A Antisocial	.33*	.20	.29	.36*	.33*	.52**	.80**	.12	.60**	.40**	.49**	.25
6B Aggressive	.25	.33*	.34*	.44**	.42**	.50**	.64**	.37*	.62**	.45**	.30*	.31*
7 Compulsive	.39**	.21	.10	.16	.31*	.43**	.39**	.49**	.40**	.44**	.31*	.37*
8A Negativistic	.34*	.48**	.60**	.62**	.38*	.42**	.56**	.14	.45**	.51**	.37*	.30*
8B Masochistic	.48**	.62**	.71**	.65**	.43**	.36*	.41**	.14	.47**	.59**	.45**	.20
S Schizotypal	.60**	.59**	.61**	.56**	.46**	.48**	.50**	.19	.44**	.76**	.61**	.43**
C Borderline	.47**	.54**	.60**	.48**	.43**	.42**	.57**	.27	.55**	.67**	.65**	.38*
P Paranoid	.52**	.49**	.39**	.46**	.59**	.57**	.47**	.38**	.50**	.68**	.41**	.55**

Schd = Schizoid;Avoid = Avoidant;Depr = Depressive; Dep = Dependent; Histr = Histrionic; Narc = Narcissistic; Antis = Antisocial; Obsess = Obsessive-Compulsive; Nega = Negativistic; Scht = Schizotypal; Bord =Borderline; Para = Paranoid. Only correlations greater than 0.60 are highlighted. * $p < 0.05$ (2-tailed) ** $p < 0.01$ (2-tailed).

Table 2. Correlations between the MCMI-III clinical scales and the PDQ-4+ scales

MCMI-III Scales	PDQ-4+ Scales											
	Schd	Avoid	Depr	Dep	Histr	Narc	Antis	Obses	Nega	Scht	Bord	Para
A Anxiety	.46**	.58**	**.69****	.60**	.47**	.37*	.50**	.20	.45**	**.72****	.56**	.34*
H Somatoform	.30*	.51**	.57**	.49**	.24	.18	.26	.14	.18	.55**	.29	.21
N Bipolar: Manic	.32*	.27	.34*	.35*	.54**	.54**	.53**	.50**	.48**	**.66****	.55**	**.52****
D Dysthymia	.40**	.57**	**.75****	.54**	.36*	.18	.30*	.12	.21	**.64****	.42**	.24
B Alcohol Dependence	.43**	.42**	.47**	.51**	.47**	.55**	**.70****	.31*	**.65****	.55**	**.64****	.36*
T Drug Dependence	.30*	.03	.12	.31*	.09	.26	**.62****	-.05	.51**	.24	.38**	.03
R Post-traumaticStress	.54**	**.60****	**.73****	**.62****	.50**	.36*	.41**	.23	.36*	**.71****	.57**	.28
SS Thought Disorder	.52**	.53**	**.63****	.51**	.52**	.48**	.49**	.30*	.45**	**.75****	**.63****	.20
CC Major Depression	.31*	.51**	**.63****	.37**	.17	.03	.23	.05	.16	.57**	.34*	.20
PP Delusional Disorder	.56**	.20	.24	.39**	**.60****	**.62****	.52**	.29	.38*	**.66****	.52**	.54**

Schd = Schizoid; Avoid = Avoidant; Depr = Depressive; Dep = Dependent; Histr = Histrionic; Narc = Narcissistic; Antis = Antisocial; Obsess = Obsessive-Compulsive; Nega = Negativistic; Scht = Schizotypal; Bord =Borderline; Para = Paranoid. Only correlations greater than 0.60 are highlighted. * p < 0.05 (2-tailed) ** p < 0.01 (2-tailed).

The Histrionic and Narcissistic PDs represented the only exceptions: in these cases, the correlations between MCMI-III and PDQ-4+ resulted not significant and very modest, respectively; this result is also consistent with that reported by Blackburn and collaborators (2004). Moreover, Widiger and Boyd (2009) examined several studies that reported convergent validity between different self-report measures for PDs and found that the lowest median values were for Compulsive and Narcissistic PDs.

The absence of association between the two scales for the Histrionic PD might be explained by the nature of the items comprising the MCMI-III Histrionic PD scale, that pertain to a larger range of attitudes and behaviors than those of PDQ-4+, which are fewer and mostly circumscribed. Specifically, the MCMI-III Histrionic PD scale's prototypical items seem to concern mainly extroverted personality, whereas non-prototypical items are mostly indicative of the absence of both introversion and depressed mood. Our results are also in line with this hypothesis, since a modest and negative correlation ($r = -.35$) between the MCMI-III Histrionic scale PD and the PDQ-4+ Depressive PD one emerged. This consideration is consistent with previous studies (Craig, 2005; Craig and Olson, 2001) that found high positive correlations between the MCMI-III Histrionic scale and items dealing with extroverted traits and ego-inflated self-evaluations and behaviors. Furthermore, it is to note that poor or absent associations between the MCMI-III Histrionic PD scale and other instruments assessing similar behavioral styles have been previously found; for example, no correlation between the MCMI-III Histrionic PD scale and the MMPI-2 Hysteria clinical scale emerged in the study by Zennaro and colleagues (2008). For these reasons, several authors (Strack, 1999; Craig and Bivens, 1998; Craig, 1999, 2005; Rossi, Andries van der Ark, and Sloore, 2007) suggested that elevated scores in the MCMI-III Histrionic PD scale might be indicative of a histrionic personality style, rather than a PD. Lastly, MCMI-III Histrionic and Narcissistic PD scales, together with the Compulsive PD one, has been found to show many similarities to the MMPI-2 measures of fake-good (Lie, Correction and Superlative Scales), revealing that they might measure socially desirable behaviors (Schoenberg, Dorr, Morgan, and Burke, 2004). In addition, the results of MCMI-III factor analysis performed by Craig and Bivens (1998) revealed that the Histrionic, Narcissistic and Compulsive PDs scales represented the negative pole of a factor named "General Maladjustment", which was peculiar to a general state of psychological disturbance characterized by depression, avoidance, detachment and low self-esteem.

A great number of associations between the MCMI-III clinical scales and the PDQ-4+ personality scales also emerged: the most relevant were those concerning mood, anxiety and psychotic disorders' symptoms, which were found to be strongly associated with Depressive and Schizotypal PDs. These results are in line with other studies and reflect the frequent comorbidities between such personality styles and clinical symptoms. For example, Carpenter, Heinrichs, and Wagman (1988) identified two different classes of symptoms in patients with schizophrenia: the former one referring to the core deficits of the disorder ("primary symptoms"); the latter one concerning secondary causes ("secondary symptoms"), which comprises anxiety, depression, social isolation and medication side effects (Carpenter et al., 1988; Kirkpatrick, Buchanan, Ross, and Carpenter, 2001). In line with this classification, Cohen and Matthews (2010) suggested the involvement of both these types of symptoms also in schizotypy. Furthermore, there is evidence supporting that psychotic disorders in general are usually characterized by a prodromal phase including symptoms as anxiety and depressed mood, thus suggesting a relationship between schizotypal characteristics, anxiety and mood disorders (Gross, 1989, 1997; Yung et al., 1996). Nonetheless, it has to be noted the great occurrence of mood, anxiety and psychotic disorders in the present sample, which may have influenced these results. Finally, the MCMI-III Alcohol Dependence scale resulted strictly related with the Borderline and Negativistic PDs scales, while both Alcohol and Drug Dependence scales were strongly associated with Antisocial PD. Such findings are in agreement with clinical and research evidence supporting the comorbidity between these personality characteristics and alcohol and drug misuse (Cohen et al., 2005; Craig, 2000; Craig, Bivens, and Olson, 1997; Echeburùa, De Medina, and Aizpiri, 2005, 2007; Grant et al., 2004; Merikangas, Swedensen, Preisig, and Chazan, 1998; Sher, Bartholow, and Wood, 2000; Vanem, Krog and Hartmann, 2008).

It deserves mention that our findings may be affected by a series of shortcomings. The main one consists in the under-representation of PDs diagnoses. Indeed, more than half participants were patients diagnosed with a mood disorder; anxiety and psychotic disorders were also particularly represented. Consequently, the second limitation regards our sample's heterogeneity. The small sample size is another important issue. Therefore, such a sample's composition does not allow to generalize present results: further studies testing both convergent validity on larger samples of patients with PDs and MCMI-III personality features among clinical groups are required. Lastly, problems concerning the Histrionic PD and Narcissistic PD scales also need to be addressed.

Even with the above-mentioned limitations, overall the present preliminary study provided data supporting good correspondences between MCMI-III and PDQ-4+ personality scales; moreover, a satisfying coherence concerning the relationship between the MCMI-III clinical symptoms and the personality characteristics as measured by the PDQ-4+ was found. Therefore, present data support the association between the Italian versions of MCMI-III and PDQ-4+.

ACKNOWLEDGMENTS

The authors wish to thank Prof. Andrea Fossati, who provided the Italian version of the PDQ-4 +.

REFERENCES

American Psychiatric Association (2000). Diagnostic and Statistical Manual of Mental Disorders, Fourth Edition, Text Revision. Washington, DC: American Psychiatric Association.

Blackburn, R., Donnelly, J.P., Logan, C., and Renwick, S.J.D. (2004). Convergent and discriminative validity of interview and questionnaire measures of personality disorder in mentally disordered offenders: A multitrait-multimethod analysis using confirmatory factor analysis. *Journal of Personality Disorders,* 18, 129-150.

Blount, C., Evans, C., Birch, F., Warren, S., and Norton, K. (2002). The properties of self-report research measures: Beyond psychometrics. *Psychology and Psychotherapy: Theory, Research and Practice,* 75, 151–164.

Boyle, G., and Le Dean, L. (2000). Discriminant Validity of the Illness Behavior Questionnaire and Millon Clinical Multiaxial Inventory-III in a Heterogeneous Sample of Psychiatric Outpatients. *Journal of Clinical Psychology,* 56, 779–791.

Butcher, J.N., Dahlstrom, W.G., Graham, J.R., Tellegen, A., and Kraemmer, B. (1989). MMPI-2: Minnesota Multiphasic Personality Inventory-2: Manual for administration and scoring. Minneapolis, MN: University of Minnesota Press.

Carpenter, W. T., Jr., Heinrichs, D. W., and Wagman, A. M. (1988). Deficit and nondeficit forms of schizophrenia: The concept. *American Journal of Psychiatry*, 145, 578–583.

Cohen, L.J., Gertmenian-King, E., Kunik, L., Weaver, C., London, E.D., and Galynker, I. (2005). Personality measures in former heroin users receiving methadone or in protracted abstinence from opiates. *Acta Psychiatrica Scandinavica,* 112, 149-158.

Cohen, A.S., and Matthews, R.A. (2010). Primary and secondary negative schizotypal traits in a large non-clinical sample. *Personality and Individual Differences,* 49, 419-424.

Craig, R.J. (1999). Overview and current status of the Millon Clinical Multiaxial Inventory. *Journal of Personality Assessment,* 72, 390-406.

Craig, R.J. (2000). Prevalence of personality disorders among cocaine and heroin addicts. *Substance Abuse*, 21, 87-94.

Craig, R.J. (2005). Alternative interpretations for the histrionic, narcissistic, and compulsive personality disorders scales of the MCMI-III. In R. J. Craig (Ed.), *New directions in interpreting the Millon Clinical Multiaxial Inventory (MCMI): Essays on current issues* (pp. 71-93). Hoboken, NJ: Wiley.

Craig, R.J., and Bivens, A. (1998). Factor structure of the MCMI-III. *Journal of Personality Assessment*, 70, 190-196.

Craig, R.J, Bivens, A., and Olson, R. (1997). MCMI-III-derived typological analysis of cocaine and heroin addicts. *Journal of Personality Assessment,* 69, 583–595.

Craig, R.J., and Olson, R.E. (2001). Adjectival descriptions of personality disorders: A convergent validity study of the MCMI-III. *Journal of Personality Assessment,* 77, 259-271.

Davison, S., Leese, M., and Taylor, P.J. (2001). Examination of the screening properties of the Personality Diagnostic Questionnaire 4+ (PDQ–4+) in a prison population. *Journal of Personality Disorders,* 15, 180-194.

Dubro, A.F., Wetzler, S., and Kahn, M.W. (1988). A comparison of three self-report questionnaires and for the diagnosis of DSM-III personality disorders. *Journal of Personality Disorders*, 2, 256-266.

Echeburùa, E., De Medina, R.B., and Aizpiri, J. (2005). Alcoholism and personality disorders: an exploratory study. *Alcohol and Alcoholism,* 40, 323-326.

Echeburùa, E., De Medina, R.B., and Aizpiri, J. (2007). Comorbidity of alcohol dependence and personality disorders: a comparative study. *Alcohol and Alcoholism,* 42, 618-622.

First, M. B., Spitzer, R. L., Gibbon, M., Williams, J. B. W., and Benjamin, L. (1996). Structured Clinical Interview for DSM-IV Axis II Personality Disorder (SCID-II). New York, NY: Biometrics Research Department New York State Psychiatric Institute.

First, M. B., Spitzer, R. L., Gibbon, M., and Williams, J. B. W. (1996). Structured Clinical Interview for DSM-IV - Patient Edition (SCID-I/P). New York: Biometrics Research Department, New York State Psychiatric Institute.

Fossati, A., Maffei, C., Bagnato, M., Donati, D., Donini, M., Fiorilli, M., Novella, L., and Ansoldi, M. (1998). Criterion validity of the Personality Diagnostic Questionnaire-41 (PDQ-41) in a mixed psychiatric sample. *Journal of Personality Disorders,* 12, 172-178.

Grant, B.F., Stinson, F.S., Dawson, D.A., Chou, S.P., Ruan, W.J., and Pickering, R.P. (2004) Co-occurrence of 12-month alcohol and drug use disorders and personality disorders in the United States. *Archives of General Psychiatry* 61, 361–368.

Gross, G. (1989). The 'basic' symptoms of schizophrenia. *British Journal of Psychiatry,* 155 (Suppl. 7), 21– 25.

Gross, G. (1997). The onset of schizophrenia. *Schizophrenia Research,* 28, 187–198.

Guthrie, P.C., and Mobley, B.D. (1994). A comparison of the differential diagnostic efficiency of three personality disorders inventories. *Journal of Clinical Psychology,* 50, 656-665.

Hicklin, J., and Widiger, T.A. (2005). Similarities and differences among antisocial and psychopathic self-report inventories from the perspective of general personality functioning. *European Journal of Personality,* 19, 325-342.

Hyler, S.E. (1994). Personality Questionnaire, PDQ-4+. New York, NY: New York State Psychiatric Institute.

Hyler, S.E., and Rieder, R.O. (1987). PDQ-R: Personality Diagnostic Questionnaire-Revised. New York, NY: New York State Psychiatric Institute.

Hyler, E.S., Skodol A.E., Oldham, J.M., Kellman H.D., and Doidge, N. (1992). Validity of the Personality Diagnostic Questionnaire-Revised: A replication in an outpatient sample. *Comprehensive Psychiatry*, 33, 73-77.

Hyler, S.E., Rieder, R.O., Spitzer, R., and Williams, J.B.W. (1983). Personality Diagnostic Questionnaire (PDQ). New York, NY: New York State Psychiatric Institute.

Kennedy, S.H., Katz, R., Rockert, W., Mendlowitz, S., Ralevski, E., and Clewes, J. (1995). Assessment of personality disorders in anorexia nervosa and bulimia nervosa. A comparison of self-report and structured interview methods. *Journal of Nervous and Mental Disease*, 183, 358-364.

Kirkpatrick, B., Buchanan, R. W., Ross, D. E., and Carpenter, W. T. Jr., (2001). A separate disease within the syndrome of schizophrenia. *Archives of General Psychiatry*, 58, 165–171.

Kim, D.I., Choi, M.R., and Cho, E.C. (2000). The preliminary study of reliability and validity on the Korean version of Personality Disorder Questionnaire-4+ (PDQ-4+). *Journal of Korean Neuropsychiatric Association*, 39, 525-538.

Lindsay, K. A., Sankis, L. M., and Widiger, T. A. (2000). Gender bias in self-report personality disorder inventories. *Journal of Personality Disorders*, 14, 218–232.

Lindsay, K.A., and Widiger, T.A. (1995). Sex and gender bias in self-report personality disorders inventories: Item analysis of the MCMI-II, MMPI and PDQ-R. *Journal of Personality Assessment*, 65, 1-20.

Marlowe, D.B., Husband, S.D., Bonieskie, L.M., Kirby, K.C., and Platt, J.J. (1997). Structured interview versus self-report test vantages for the assessment of personality pathology in cocaine dependence. *Journal of Personality Disorders*, 11,177-90.

Merikangas, K.R., Swedensen, J.D., Preisig, M.A., and Chazan, R.Z. (1998). Psychopathology and temperament in parents and offspring: Results of a family study. *Journal of Affective Disorders*, 51,63-74.

Messina, N., Wish, E., Hoffman, J., and Nemes, S. (2001). Diagnosing antisocial personality disorder among substance abusers: the SCID versus the MCMI-II. *American Journal of Drug and Alcohol Abuse*, 27, 699-717.

Millon, T. (1983). Millon Clinical Multiaxial Inventory. Minneapolis, MN: National Computer Systems.

Millon, T. (1987). Manual for the MCMI-II (2nd edition). Minneapolis, MN: National Computer Systems.

Millon, T. (1996). An evolutionary theory of personality disorders. J.F. Clarkin and M.F. Lenzenweger (Eds). *Major theories of personality disorder* (pp. 221-346). New York, NY: Guilford Press.

Millon, T., Davis, R.D., and Millon, C. (1997). Manual for the Millon Clinical Multiaxial Inventory-III (MCMI-III), Second Edition. Minneapolis, MN: National Computer Systems.

Reich, J., and Troughton, E. (1988). Frequency of DSM-III personality disorders in patients with panic disorder: comparison with psychiatric and normal control subjects. *Psychiatry Research*, 26, 89-100.

Rossi, G., Andries van der Ark, L., and Sloore, H. (2007). Factor analysis of the Dutch-Language version of the MCMI-III. *Journal of Personality Assessment,* 88, 144-157.

Schoenberg, M.R., Dorr, D., Morgan, C.D., and Burke, M. (2004). A comparison of the MCMI-III personality disorder and modifier indices with the MMPI-2 clinical and validity scales. *Journal of Personality Assessment*, 82, 273-280.

Sher, K.H., Bartholow, B.D., and Wood, M.D. (2000). Personality and substance use disorders: A prospective study. *Journal of Consulting and Clinical Psychology*, 68, 818-829.

Skodol, A.E., and Bender, D.S. (2009). The Future of Personality Disorders in DSM-V? *American Journal of Psychiatry*, 166, 388-391.

Spitzer, R.L. (1983). Psychiatric diagnosis: are clinicians still necessary? *Comprehensive Psychiatry*, 24, 399-411.

Strack, S. (1999). Millon's normal personality styles and dimensions. *Journal of Personality Assessment*, 72, 426-436.

Vanem, P.C., Krog, D., and Hartmann, E. (2008). Assessment of substance abusers on the MCMI-III and the Rorschach. *Scandinavian Journal of Psychology*, 49, 83-91.

Widiger, T.A., and Boyd, S. (2009). Assessing personality disorders. In: J.N. Butcher (editor). *Oxford handbook of personality assessment.* 3rd edition, pp. 336–363. New York, NY: Oxford University Press.

Widiger, T.A., and Samuel, D.B. (2005). Evidence-based assessment of personality disorders. *Psychological Assessment*, 17, 278-287.

Wilberg, T., Dammen, T., and Friis, S. (2000). Comparing Personality Diagnostic Questionnaire-4+ with Longitudinal, Expert, All Data (LEAD) Standard Diagnoses in a sample with a high prevalence of Axis I and Axis II disorders. *Comprehensive Psychiatry*, 41, 295-302.

Yang, J., McCrae, R.R., Costa, P.T., Yao, S., Dai, X., Cai, T., and Gao., B. (2000). The cross-cultural generalizability of Axis-II constructs: An evaluation of two personality disorder assessment instruments in the People's Republic of China. *Journal of Personality Disorders*, 14, 249-263.

Yung, A.R., McGorry, P.D., McFarlane, C.A., Jackson, H.J., Patton, G.C., and Rakkar, A. (1996). Monitoring and care of young people at incipient risk of psychosis. *Schizophrenia Bullettin,* 22, 283–303.

Zennaro, A., Ferracuti, S., Lang, M., and Sanavio, E. (2008). Adattamento italiano del MCMI-III: studi di validazione. Firenze: Giunti Organizzazioni Speciali.

INDEX

U

V

T

W

Y